A CRITICAL COMPANION TO
ANCIENT ALIENS
SEASONS 3 AND 4

UNAUTHORIZED

A CRITICAL COMPANION TO
ANCIENT ALIENS
SEASONS 3 AND 4

UNAUTHORIZED

Jason Colavito

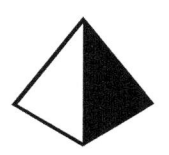

· JASONCOLAVITO.COM ·
· ALBANY, NEW YORK · 2012 ·

Copyright © 2012 by Jason Colavito

Published by Jason Colavito, Albany, New York

All Rights Reserved. No part of this book may be reproduced or transmitted by any means, electronic or mechanical, including photocopy, recording, or any other information storage and retrieval system, in any form whatsoever (except for copying permitted by U.S. copyright law or by reviewers for the public press), without the express written permission of the author.

Versions of the material included in this book first appeared on JasonColavito.com.

This book is not produced or endorsed by *Ancient Aliens: The Series*, Prometheus Entertainment, or A&E Television Networks.

This book has been typeset in Charis SIL

ISBN: 978-1-300-09302-2

www.JasonColavito.com

CONTENTS

PREFACE — vii
INTRODUCTION — ix

SEASON THREE

1. ALIENS AND THE OLD WEST &
7. ALIENS, PLAGUES, AND EPIDEMICS — 1
   COMMENTARY: ETHICS AND ANCIENT ALIENS — 5
   COMMENTARY: ETHICS AND ANCIENT ALIENS PART II — 9

5. ALIENS AND MYSTERIOUS RITUALS — 13
   COMMENTARY: SERIOUSLY, YOU THINK CROWNS COME FROM ALIENS STANDING IN SUNSHINE? — 15

8. ALIENS AND LOST WORLDS — 19
   EPISODE REVIEW — 21
   COMMENTARY: DAMN THOSE LYING ANCIENT TEXTS! — 24

9. ALIENS AND DEADLY WEAPONS — 31
   EPISODE REVIEW — 33

3. ALIENS AND SACRED PLACES &
10. ALIENS AND EVIL PLACES — 39
    EPISODE REVIEW — 41

11. ALIENS AND THE FOUNDING FATHERS — 45
    EPISODE REVIEW — 47

12. ALIENS AND DEADLY CULTS — 49
    EPISODE REVIEW — 51

13. ALIENS AND THE SECRET CODE — 55
    EPISODE REVIEW — 57

14. ALIENS AND THE UNDEAD — 61
    EPISODE REVIEW — 63

15. ALIENS, GODS, AND HEROES — 65
    EPISODE REVIEW — 67

16. ALIENS AND THE CREATION OF MAN — 71
    EPISODE REVIEW — 73

SEASON FOUR

1. THE MAYAN CONSPIRACY — 79
   EPISODE REVIEW — 81

2. THE DOOMSDAY PROPHECIES — 89
   EPISODE REVIEW — 91

3. THE GREYS — 99
   EPISODE REVIEW — 101

4. ALIENS AND MEGA-DISASTERS — 109
   EPISODE REVIEW — 111

5. THE NASA CONNECTION — 117
   EPISODE REVIEW — 119

6. THE MYSTERIES OF PUMA PUNKU — 125
   EPISODE REVIEW — 127

7. ALIENS AND BIGFOOT — 135
   EPISODE REVIEW — 137

8. THE DA VINCI CONSPIRACY — 147
   EPISODE REVIEW — 149

9. THE TIME TRAVELERS — 155
   EPISODE REVIEW — 157
   COMMENTARY: INVESTIGATING BIBLICAL TIME TRAVEL — 165

10. ALIENS AND DINOSAURS — 169
    EPISODE REVIEW — 171

    APPENDIX: RÉSUMÉS OF THE GODS — 179
    INDEX — 183

PREFACE

As the History Channel (and later H2) program *Ancient Aliens: The Series* grew in popularity and cultural impact over its first two seasons, I occasionally wrote about its strange assertions and outright fabrications on my JasonColavito.com blog. I had written the 2005 book *The Cult of Alien Gods: H. P. Lovecraft and Extraterrestrial Pop Culture* about ancient astronaut believers and had covered alternative theories in *Skeptic* magazine since 2004. However, I did not write often about the program due to its depiction of my work in its 2009 pilot episode (see pages xv and 9). I did not want to give publicity to a program that had treated me poorly.

But during the third season of the show I began to seriously review the program on an episode-by-episode basis after I discovered how many people were taking the program very seriously and how few were systematically challenging its assertions. At the height of its popularity, two million Americans watched *Ancient Aliens: The Series* each week, an astonishing number.

What you are about to read is a collection of my episode reviews and commentaries covering Seasons 3 and 4 of *Ancient Aliens*. This material first appeared on my blog in 2011 and 2012 and is presented here largely as originally written, with minimal revisions for consistency and to adapt the blog format for print. My early commentaries addressed elements of the first few episodes of season 3, and my full episode reviews began with Season 3, episode 8 and continued uninterrupted until the end of Season 4.

INTRODUCTION
MY ALIEN AFTERNOON WITH GIORGIO TSOUKALOS

WHENEVER I SEE *Ancient Aliens* come on the History Channel or H2 and hear the emphatically-emphasized exclamations of "ancient astronaut theorist" Giorgio A. Tsoukalos, a consulting producer on the show, I can't help but flash back to the time I interviewed him, a long time ago, with repercussions echoing down the years. It's a story I've never told in full, largely because until recently Tsoukalos wasn't famous enough prior to *Ancient Aliens* to make the story worth telling, and I had no reason to want to make a bad situation worse. In my *Cult of Alien Gods* (2005), I gave a brief, expurgated account of the story in a footnote. But this is what really happened.

I was standing in Giorgio Tsoukalos's spacious living room, marveling at its tall, floor-to-ceiling bookcases groaning under the weight of literature—mostly, but not entirely, works of "alternative" history and the ancient astronaut theory—Erich von Däniken, Robert Charroux, Zecharia Sitchin, David Childress, and more. I fiddled with my red tie, adjusting it against my deep blue dress shirt. I didn't wear ties often enough to feel entirely comfortable. I looked around the room.

One side of the room was decorated in ancient chic: reproductions of Egyptian and African artifacts, globes and maps. The other side of the room, leading toward the front door of the low-slung house nestled on a forested street, was hung with posters of well-muscled men, mementos from Tsoukalos' then-career as a body-building promoter. Tsoukalos himself was all smiles, his tall black hair not yet grown to the prodigious height now so well-known.

Dressed casually in a blue oxford and chinos, he seemed youthful and ebullient.

I was a college student a few weeks shy of 21, young and arrogant but already disillusioned with college life. I had realized that I had chosen my major and my career path poorly, and it was time for a change. It was the early spring of 2002, and this would be one of the last pieces I would create as a student of television journalism. I would finish out the degree, but I added to it a second major in anthropology, which suited me somewhat better.

With me were two other students, Nikolai and Josh, and they fiddled with the camera—and ancient, heavy model that recorded on videocassette—and worked to set up the three point lighting in the space Tsoukalos had cleared out in front of his desk, with a dramatic backdrop of his books. From the right angle, it would look as though his library went on forever.

How lucky, I thought, that the head of the Archaeology, Aeronautics, and SETI Research Association (AAS-RA, now called the Ancient Alien Society), lived here in Ithaca, N.Y., only a couple of miles down the hill from my college dorm. I recalled how exciting it was to discover this fact during a then-novel bout of internet research, and how I had pushed my teammates to agree to a profile of Tsoukalos for our Television Journalism Workshop project when it was my turn to play "reporter" and serve as the on-camera personality. In retrospect, it was already obvious that I had lost my love for journalism and was trying to keep myself interested by pushing for stories that overlapped my extracurricular interests.

So here I was sitting across from Giorgio Tsoukalos preparing to ask him questions about the ancient astronaut theory. Tsoukalos reminded me twice before we started that he had been interviewed on NBC and the Sci-Fi Channel (now SyFy), and it was a great boon that a worldly entrepreneur and scholar would choose to speak to students. Tsoukalos was, and remains, just three years older than me. He and I had attended the same school, Ithaca College, where he earned a 1998 bachelor's in sports information communication.

I knew none of this in 2002; instead, I knew Tsoukalos only as the Swiss-Greek head of the AAS-RA, and so I started to ask him questions about the ancient astronaut theory. I wish I remember exactly what I asked, but when I checked my notes from that spring, I found that the interview made so little impression at the time that I recorded nothing about it, unusual since I was typically a faithful recorder of scholastic events. I do know that the interview went badly. Since I was at the end of my studies of TV journalism, I had no compunction about using the interview to challenge Tsoukalos on facts and theories, and I recall that the interview grew heated. The smile fell from Tsoukalos's face, and he repeated several talking points and referred me to ancient astronaut literature. This I remember very clearly: Ending the interview, Tsoukalos reminded me again that he had been on NBC and Sci-Fi and had never once been challenged on a single claim or point. *Why*, he asked, *do you think you, a student, can do that to me?*

I smoothed things over, or so I thought, explaining to Tsoukalos that what I was doing was "news" reporting, and what the Sci-Fi Channel did was not news. I told him that I was following Lawrence Spivak's maxim that a good interview involves learning everything about the interviewee's subject and then taking the other side. We parted company on polite terms, the near-permanent grin etching itself back across his face. He asked me to give him a copy of the interview tape for his archive, and I told him he could have one after the project was finished.

In the car on the ride back up the hill to campus, Nikolai and Josh congratulated me on the interview. They thought I "got him good" and greatly enjoyed my performance. But that was what it was—a performance. There was already tension between my false face of objective journalism, which needed to pretend that the ancient astronaut theory is the "other side" of the story, and the skeptical critic I was slowly but surely becoming. This day, I got the balance wrong, and I was a skeptic pretending to be a journalist. It wasn't fair, I suppose, to come to Tsoukalos's house as a "journalist" and then argue with him as a skeptic. But I was not quite 21 and did not yet understand this; he was 24 and was equally bull-headed and confrontational.

The difference between us became more obvious over the coming weeks and years. The final tape of the story came together badly. In those days Ithaca College still used giant, room-sized machines to splice and edit physical video tape—the digital revolution had not yet filtered down to us. The final copy of the story was grainy and blurry. Some of the cuts went badly, and the audio levels were too high in places, and then too low in others. I had trouble, too, writing a script that "fairly" reported Tsoukalos's views, as though they were equal to the scientific view, the "other side." To finish off the humiliation, after playing the story for my professor, the master tape broke. My partners and I wrote it off as a loss, and someone (I can't remember which of us) threw the tape away rather than waste time reserving an editing booth and manually splicing together a video no one would ever watch again. The piece was never broadcast anywhere; it was merely a class exercise. We needed to start on the next assignment.

Unfortunately, I had forgotten that I had promised Giorgio Tsoukalos a copy of the tape. A few weeks later, he emailed me asking for a copy. I tried to be polite, and I explained to him that due to a mishap the tape had unfortunately broken. I reminded him what I had explained before our interview, that it was a class assignment and was not intended to air. Tsoukalos did not believe me, and after several email exchanges, he more or less accused me of rank dishonesty, and worse; I am sure I responded in kind, sure I would never see him again. Eventually, after weeks of emails, he gave up and realized no tape was forthcoming. But he never forgave me.

In late 2003, after I had graduated from Ithaca College, I started work on what would become my article "Charioteer of the Gods," and then the book *The Cult of Alien Gods*. I somehow still felt the weight of my journalism training, and I felt that as part of my research, I needed to speak with ancient astronaut authors to interview them about their beliefs and my thesis. I reached out to Erich von Däniken, the author of *Chariots of the Gods*, and the wellspring of the modern ancient astronaut theory. Unfortunately, unbeknownst to me, Giorgio Tsoukalos was now von Däniken's gatekeeper and official English-language representative.

On July 29, 2003, Tsoukalos wrote back in response to my email to von Däniken. He began by asking if I were surprised that he, not von Däniken, was writing. He reminded me that my bad behavior the year before had serious consequences. He then "answered" my question on von Däniken's behalf:

Just the fact that you so desperately attempt to dismantle our theory *proves* that we *are* on the *right* track. Otherwise you would *not* feel so threatened by our theories! ... I will certainly not forward your questions to Erich, and his secretary has already been informed about your malevolent intentions.

Tsoukalos went on to "inform" his other friends of my "malevolent" intentions (he always liked grandiose words), including David Hatcher Childress, a "lost civilizations scholar" and advocate of Lemuria, Mu, and some mystical claptrap called the "Rama Empire." In solidarity with Tsoukalos, Childress developed an extreme reaction to me, especially after reading the articles I wrote about his theories on my first website, and later in *Cult*. We have never met.

Years later, in 2006, Childress still loathed me and told a reporter for *The Chicago Reader* that I grossly misrepresented him. In a private conversation that I suppose I shouldn't mention except that it wasn't technically "off the record," the reporter explained to me that Childress considered me a nemesis, and I was the first name on his lips when asked about writers who opposed his views. Childress told the reporter that I was wrong because he was not an ancient astronaut theorist and therefore my book was a fraud:

> [M]y whole thing is that this stuff is from this planet. These giant ruins aren't built by extraterrestrials. I say they were built by humans. Mankind and civilization goes back 50,000 years or more. What else can I assume is inaccurate in this book [*Cult of Alien Gods*]? This guy just plain doesn't do his research.

In the spring of 2010, Childress began appearing weekly on the History Channel's (now H2's) *Ancient Aliens: The Series*, along with his friend Giorgio Tsoukalos, billed now as an "ancient astronaut theorist." He can now be found each week explaining that "the aliens" are responsible for archaeological and geological wonders. In one episode he explained that the aliens used satellites to beam electricity from Egyptian obelisks across the Pacific to move Easter Island's statues. He claimed the aliens gave the Maya rockets.

When Childress and Tsoukalos filmed the pilot episode of *Ancient Aliens* in 2009, the producers from Prometheus Entertainment asked them for skeptics whose work they could show to illustrate attacks on the ancient astronaut theory. Naturally, they thought of me—the only skeptic whose name appears in the segment as broadcast. And so, there I am in the pilot episode of the series, my name clearly visible in large print from my 2004 article "Charioteer of the Gods," sliding across the screen to ominous music as a wicked, evil skeptic. A friend of my father's called my father during the broadcast, excited to see my name and wondering why it had been inverted into white type on black paper, with burning scare quotes scrawled across my article of insults hurled against alien theorists—scare quotes I never said. I wasn't sure whether it was humiliating to be attacked on national television or a badge of honor. I lean now toward the latter.

And so, nearly a decade later, long after a heated, unseen interview in an Ithaca living room, ancient astronaut theorists still hold a grudge against me and probably will for life. But I have Giorgio Tsoukalos to thank for one thing. Though I did not recognize it at the time, my interview with him showed me that I am not cut out for the false equivalences of so much of contemporary journalism. I cannot lie and pretend that falsehoods are equal to facts. For whatever reason, one random college assignment inadvertently determined the path my future would take.

ANCIENT ALIENS
SEASON THREE

EPISODE 1:
ALIENS AND THE OLD WEST
JULY 28, 2011

&

EPISODE 7:
ALIENS, PLAGUES, AND EPIDEMICS
SEPTEMBER 8, 2011

COMMENTARY
ETHICS AND ANCIENT ALIENS

IN LATE JULY 2011, when *Cowboys & Aliens*, a major studio movie about gold-hungry aliens invading the Old West, was new in theaters, *Ancient Aliens*, then airing on the History Channel, devoted an hour to "Aliens and the Old West." This was the first episode of the show's third season. Not coincidentally, the show used clips from the movie as a springboard for some (very) tangentially related speculation about extraterrestrial visitation in the Old West, lands abutting the Old West, lands on the same continent as the Old West, and places that simply existed at the same time as the Old West, c. 1850 to 1910. (I've never thought of Ohio as the Old West, but what do I know?)

In early September 2011, the killer-virus movie *Contagion* hit theaters, and—surprise of surprises--*Ancient Aliens* had an hour on aliens and, yes, killer viruses, speculating that extraterrestrials were behind a series of devastating ancient plagues. Needless to say, the hour was complete nonsense (the connection is that ancient people blamed the gods for disease, and the gods were "really" aliens, so aliens cause disease); however, that is merely par for the course with the sorry excuse for a "documentary" series. But unlike the earlier *Cowboys*-themed episode, the virus edition did not include promotional material for or scenes from the movie *Contagion*.

The bigger question is this: How can we trust a program that is allegedly presenting serious truths when these supposedly nonfiction truths are carefully manipulated to coincide with Hollywood's movie release schedule?

In the case of most entertainment programs, this is not much of an issue. When the History Channel does a program on *Angels and Demons Decoded* (2009) or *Indiana Jones and the Ultimate Quest* (2008), the viewer pretty much knows what he or she is in for: bought and paid for movie-based infotainment with a few "real life" facts added in.

But *Ancient Aliens* purports to be an actual, independent, serious documentary series exploring the ancient astronaut theory, which pays lip service to being "scientific." If we assume for even a moment that there is any merit in the ancient astronaut theory, we should be deeply disturbed by the idea that producers at Prometheus Entertainment and executives at the History Channel are willing to alter, manipulate, and selectively present facts and evidence in service of Hollywood's promotional agenda.

On *Coast to Coast AM* on July 31, 2011, *Ancient Aliens* talking head Giorgio Tsoukalos and *Coast to Coast AM* host George Noory described the "Aliens and the Old West" program as an official *Cowboys & Aliens* movie "tie-in." It appears that money exchanged hands between *Ancient Aliens* and *Cowboys & Aliens* to secure the inclusion of scenes from the movie in the documentary program. *Cowboys & Aliens* was produced by Universal Studios, which is owned by NBCUniversal, a 15% owner of the History Channel.

Now, take into consideration the explicit aim of the ancient astronaut theorists and their organization, the Archaeology, Astronautics and SETI Research Organization (AAS-RA), later renamed the Ancient Alien Society, according to Giorgio Tsoukalos himself:

> The A.A.S. R.A. is determined to prove, using scientific research methods, but in 'layman's terms,' as to whether or not extraterrestrials have visited Earth in the remote past. [...] We work along the same lines as

conventional science does, but we take it one step further: the A.A.S.R.A. takes into consideration ALL discoveries and information from ALL fields of science.[1]

So-called "conventional science" has strict ethics policies designed to avoid conflicts of interest, or to disclose them when they occur. It is the only way to judge whether results can be trusted to be honest and fairly reported, and even then the system does not always work. The National Academy of Sciences defines conflict of interest as:

> any financial or other interest which conflicts with the service of the individual because it (1) could significantly impair the individual's objectivity or (2) could create an unfair competitive advantage for any person or organization.

I would think that using a supposedly factual documentary program as a paid advertisement for a Hollywood film would meet the conflict of interest definition as given above. *Ancient Aliens* did not disclose any financial relationship during the July 28 broadcast (though legal details were provided in the end credits), nor did they acknowledge or explain how closely the program worked with the movie to develop an hour providing "real life" material to support the film's fictional storyline. Were movie producers involved in selecting material to include? Did they have editorial control over the final product?

As for the talking heads on the show: How much did the ancient alien theorists on the program know? Did producers inform them

---

[1] This and other AAS-RA writings were removed from Legendary-Times.com shortly after I cited them on my JasonColavito.com blog.

that their speculations were to be used to promote a film? If so, did this affect their views or cause them to alter their speculations to conform to the Hollywood storyline?

For ancient astronaut theorists who claim that they are true scientists and who claim that those working in the sciences are engaged in a conspiracy for profit to suppress ancient astronaut findings, this kind of conflict of interest in unconscionable. But for "entertainers," this sort of close cross-promotional relationship is standard operating procedure.

Ancient astronaut theorists and I will always disagree on the interpretation of the facts (and, as I have shown, whether there are any "facts" at all), but now I must seriously question their most basic motivations. Are they honestly deluded, or do they simply weave speculation to order for cash?

If it's the latter, I'd like to take up a collection to pay them to shut up.

COMMENTARY
ETHICS AND ANCIENT ALIENS PART II

In the preceding essay, I examined a question of journalistic ethics surrounding *Ancient Aliens*, which purports to be a "documentary" series. The July 28, 2011 broadcast, "Aliens and the Old West," featured a movie tie-in with *Cowboys & Aliens* from the History Channel's corporate cousin, Universal Studios, but the program did not acknowledge this relationship or explain how closely the program's producers and talking heads worked with the movie's marketing campaign.

This raised questions about the objectivity of the program, and whether those involved purposely manipulated their supposedly scientific theories to work with the movie's marketing machine. One piece of evidence in favor of that hypothesis is the program's strange effort to reclassify Ohio and Illinois as "the Old West," suggesting that producers purposely manipulated or altered a previously-planned program to conform to the movie's theme.

I would like to discuss this a little more.

Of course, I have no knowledge of the internal workings of Prometheus Entertainment, the production company behind *Ancient Aliens*, so I do not know what really happened. As of this writing, Prometheus Entertainment did not respond to my repeated requests for information or comment.

Prometheus also failed to respond in 2009 when I requested comment after they digitally manipulated material bearing my name to give a negative impression of me during the pilot episode of *Ancient Aliens*, unfairly associating me with others' intemperate slurs directed against ancient astronaut theorists.

10 A Critical Companion to ANCIENT ALIENS

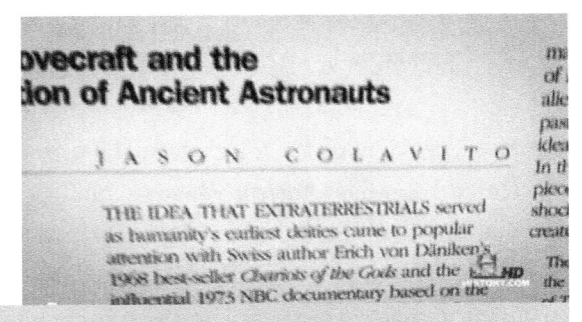

> **ovecraft and the
> ion of Ancient Astronauts**
>
> JASON COLAVITO
>
> THE IDEA THAT EXTRATERRESTRIALS served as humanity's earliest deities came to popular attention with Swiss author Erich von Däniken's 1968 best-seller *Chariots of the Gods* and the influential 1973 NBC documentary based on the

"But in spite of the book's enormous popularity— or perhaps because of it, von Däniken's theories were scorned by scientists, and jeered at by theologians." Narration over my name, *Ancient Aliens* pilot, 2009

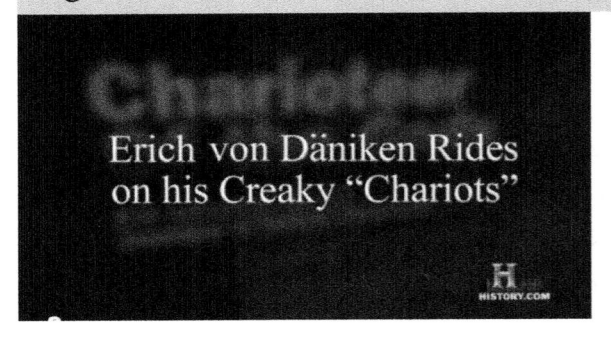

Erich von Däniken Rides on his Creaky "Chariots"

Founded in 1999, Prometheus Entertainment is the production company behind E!'s *Kendra* and the Travel Channel's *Food Paradise*. It is explicitly dedicated to "docudramas" (reality shows) and "imaginative and informative non-fiction series"—pointedly *not* programs that are expected to conform to traditional journalistic or documentary ethics. Interestingly, however, Prometheus was the production company behind *Star Wars: The Legacy Revealed* (2007), another movie tie-in special broadcast on the History Channel.

As of this writing, ancient astronaut theorist Giorgio Tsoukalos still refers to himself as a "consulting producer" on *Ancient Aliens*, further raising questions about whether the ancient alien theorists on the program altered their views to conform to *Cowboys & Aliens*' marketing needs, and whether Tsoukalos, as a "consulting producer," agreed to and approved any plan to use *Ancient Aliens* as a marketing vehicle.

According to the Center for Social Media, documentary filmmaking for cable television has raised concerns in recent years due to a perceived erosion of ethical standards as the number of hours of original program grows:

> ...many of the filmmakers surveyed spoke of commercial pressures, particularly in the cable business, to make decisions they believed to be unethical. The trend towards faster and cheaper documentaries and the "assembly line" nature of work has proven challenging to filmmakers' understanding of their obligations to subjects in particular.[2]

Further, the Center found that most television networks have standards designed to place factual integrity above marketing pressures:

> The standards and practices share some common themes, as analyzed by project advisor Jon Else. They typically assert that an independent media is a bulwark of democracy, and that the trust—of both audience and subject—is essential. They eschew conflict of interest.[3]

---

[2] Patricia Aufderheide, Peter Jaszi, and Mridu Chandra, "Honest Truths: Documentary Filmmakers on Ethical Challenges in Their Work," *Center for Social Media*, 2009 <http://www.centerforsocialmedia.org>

[3] Ibid.

Now in most cases a stupid cable documentary about aliens would hardly seem worth staging a fight over about ethical standards. Few viewers likely expect the highest levels of journalistic, documentary, or scientific ethics from *Ancient Aliens*.

But this program claims to be different from mere entertainment programs. Its talking heads, including "consulting producer" Tsoukalos, claim that they are attempting to overturn scientific paradigms about the human past while acting in the interest of science: "We work along the same lines as conventional science does," Tsoukalos wrote. "We approach our research objectively and without bias."

Does that objectivity extend to Tsoukalos' television work? How can viewers be sure that what they hear is presented "objectively" and "without bias" when the program Tsoukalos "produces" is involved in a marketing campaign for an entertainment product, one that has a vested interest in pretending that aliens really ran around the Old West?

EPISODE 5:
ALIENS AND MYSTERIOUS RITUALS
AUGUST 25, 2011

COMMENTARY
SERIOUSLY, YOU THINK CROWNS CAME FROM ALIENS STANDING IN SUNSHINE?

During the course of "Aliens and Mysterious Rituals," Giorgio Tsoukalos made a claim that is stupid even by that show's lax intellectual standards. The episode focused on the "alien" origin of religious rituals and religious and royal symbols and iconography. Tsoukalos argued that aliens wore space suits that were very similar to those worn by Apollo astronauts, and therefore the origin of royal crowns happened when ancient people—and I am not making this up—saw the astronauts stand in front of the sun with the light reflecting and bouncing off the helmets of the astronauts. He also thought that aliens using "flashlights" could produce the same effect artificially. Awed and confused, ancient humans then assumed the aliens emitted light from their heads and therefore imitated the extraterrestrials by making gold halos for their own heads.

It boggles the mind that Tsoukalos has such a low opinion of ancient intelligence that he seriously thinks prehistoric people failed to understand that when someone stands in front of the sun, it looks like he or she has a glow around his or her head.

How do we know this isn't true? Well, here is some ancient art. On the next page, you'll see a depiction of Helios, the Greek god of the sun, from an ancient temple.

As should be fairly obvious, the lines around Helios' head are the rays of the sun. Clearly, the Greeks and Romans understood the idea of the sun and how it looked around a person's head. But they are relatively late. Do we have something older? Why, yes.

Metope of Helios from the Temple of Athena, Troy. (Wikimedia Commons)

Here is the ancient Egyptian sun-god Ra crowned with the sun. The Egyptians seemed to have a pretty good grasp on the concept of the sun and knew it when they saw it.

Ra, crowned with sun, in solar barque. (Wikimedia Commons)

What we think of today as a "crown" differs from traditional headdresses worn by ancient monarchs. The modern crown derives from two sources: the sun-beam diadem worn by the priests of Sol Invictus in ancient Rome, which was worn by the Roman emperor in the imperial period, and the gold circle, or diadem, worn by the Persian emperors and adopted by Constantine as a replacement for the pagan headgear. This diadem, in turn, was a metallic version of what was originally a silk ribbon that connoted royal authority and was wrapped around a conical tiara, itself derived from earlier Mesopotamian tiaras that originated as decorated hats.

In neither case did the crown "imitate" alien helmet reflections. There is no need for such silliness when there are clear antecedents from documented historical periods that prove the origins of the crown. Sol (Helios) was admitted to be the sun, so he can be no misunderstanding of alien helmet reflections, and the diadem and tiara had mundane origins in shawls and hats worn for thousands of years to, ironically, protect the head from the sun.

Need proof that the tiara was a glorified hat and not an alien artifact? At right is the ancient Babylonian ruler Hammurabi (c. 1750 BCE) wearing a domed crown while the sun god Shamash wears a conical tiara

Stella of Hammurabi (standing), now in the Louvre. (Wikimedia Commons)

that looks like neither a space helmet nor a sun beam, but rather an ice cream cone or sea shell.

As Gwendolyn Leick noted in *The Babylonians: An Introduction* (2003), a wide array of hats were worn in that ancient empire, from turbans and fezzes to the tall, conical crowns of the monarch (p. 137). They were not, however, typically gold in color, nor did they represent the sun. In other words, the size and shape of the hat evolved from the need to show off and proclaim one's importance, not because an alien stood in front of the sun.

Of course we can't prove that the idea for wearing a hat didn't originate in a cave person seeing an alien standing before the sun and thinking, "Maybe I should put big gold triangles in my hair and hold them on with a metal circle." But the weight of the evidence suggests that this hypothesis can better be explained through the simple process of cultural evolution from practical hats to elaborate, impractical crowns meant to distinguish the idle elite from the common working person.

EPISODE 8:
ALIENS AND LOST WORLDS
SEPTEMBER 15, 2011

EPISODE REVIEW

THIS EPISODE of *Ancient Aliens* was remarkably subdued, with rather few completely outrageous claims. Instead, this episode focused more on silly interpretations of actual facts, relying on real archaeologists to present those facts before speculating those facts into oblivion. Fortunately, the final act provides another wonderful example of how ancient astronaut theorists contradict themselves. I will discuss that example later as a separate essay. First, let's discuss the rest of the episode.

The program, devoted to "Aliens and Lost Worlds," purported to explore ancient ruins around the world for their connection to alien gods, mostly by saying that Mayan carvings "look like" aliens in space suits or, in the vaguely colonialist words of ancient astronaut theorist David Hatcher Childress, art from some "oriental country" (well, which is it?) and then speculating that aliens flew serpent-shaped airplanes between China and Central America to—what exactly?—share sculpting tips? Aliens, of course, distributed art styles mostly at random, just to confuse archaeologists. Otherwise the "alien style" would be all too obvious!

It also included a dismissive segment claiming, according to *Coast to Coast AM* host George Noory, that "nobody has the answer" to how and why the Easter Island statues were moved, ignoring the recent work of Terry Hunt and Carl Lipo that proposed one, albeit controversial, solution the mystery in *The Statues that Walked* (2011). Ancient astronaut theorist Giorgio Tsoukalos, the aliens gave the islanders super-technology to move the statues, even though they can be (and were) moved with wood. But by their standards these were rather minor transgressions, more ignorant than outright fabricated.

On the plus side, that chameleon writer David Childress finally gave up any pretense of pretending he isn't an ancient astronaut theorist and spent all of his screen time talking about the "space visitors."

Nevertheless, there were a few particularly awful outrages this week. In discussing the magi who visited the infant Christ, Tsoukalos sought to link them to a worldwide secret cult of alien-worshipers:

> ...according to the ancient texts, it was the initiates of each culture who were in touch with extraterrestrials, and it was the initiates who later became priests or magi.

How does one even begin to unpack a sentence as full of assumptions as that one? Here, Tsoukalos has again taken "ancient texts" as a unified whole, a single program of textual production stretching from the dawn of writing c. 3000 BCE all the way down to the medieval period, four thousand or so years later. What he means by "initiates" is not clear, but from the context he appears to be stating a tautology: Initiates are those who are initiated into the rites of the gods and are therefore by definition close to their gods. He then assumes that 1) the gods are aliens, 2) the aliens came to earth in flesh-and-blood form, 3) humans met with, communicated with, and received wisdom from these aliens, and 4) humans mistook aliens for gods. Then, to make things even more tenuous, he suggests that those who met with the aliens established—in every earth culture, over four millennia or more—priesthoods to preserve the aliens' memory. That is an astonishing number of fact-free assumptions for a single sentence presented as established fact.

Back in the 1960s, in *Chariots of the Gods?*, Erich von Däniken proposed that the lines scratched in the Nazca desert of Peru were UFO runways: "Seen from the air, the clear-cut impression that the 37-mile-long plain of Nazca made on me was that of an airfield! What is so far-fetched about the idea?" One must give the man credit. More than forty years later, and despite decades of archaeological research into the Nazca lines—and the complete lack of evidence for any alien visitation—he stuck to his story on *Ancient Aliens*:

> In the beginning, there were (sic) just one line made by some robot or some extraterrestrial spaceship or some space shuttle because they were looking for raw material for energy.

Of course, since von Däniken realized that rockets don't need runways, the original theory has been tweaked some. Back in the 1960s von Däniken's aliens were all about reproduction, colonization, and dominance, reflecting the political concerns of Cold War Europe and its crumbling colonial empires. Today's version, however, is now about "energy" in an era that is concerned with global warming and alternative energy sources.

Finally, the episode concludes with a (mostly) sober discussion of the search for the Garden of Eden, which goes off the rails when the program (correctly) links the Biblical account to ancient Mesopotamian mythic traditions and then (wrongly) attributes those myths to aliens. This will be the subject of my next essay.

COMMENTARY
DAMN THOSE LYING ANCIENT TEXTS!

I HAVE FREQUENTLY DISCUSSED the elastic definition of "ancient texts" employed by *Ancient Aliens* and the ancient astronaut theorists (AATs) who appear on the program, especially Giorgio Tsoukalos, the publisher of the ancient astronaut journal *Legendary Times* and a consulting producer on the series. In this essay, I'd like to look at the use of a specific set of "ancient texts" in the ancient astronaut theory in order to show the way AATs somehow manage to undercut their own theory due to their misunderstanding or ignorance of the ancient texts they purport to cite.

Our example comes from "Aliens and Lost Worlds." In the final third of the program, the documentary went in search of the alien origins of the Garden of Eden. In so doing, it drew on the now-common knowledge that the biblical narrative finds its origin in Mesopotamian mythology, which included an earthly paradise.

The program then went on to discuss the Sumerian gods, including those who were present at the creation of humanity. As related by the narrator of the program, the Sumerian gods known as the "Anunnaki" were really "an alien race," according, once again, to those all-important ancient texts. These texts are cited simply as "Sumerian cuneiform tablets."

These Anunnaki were made famous in ancient astronaut circles through the work of Zecharia Sitchin, whose eccentric interpretations of Near Eastern texts transformed the high gods of Mesopotamia into a race of aliens who lived on a wandering planet and lusted after earth's gold. But the idea of the Sumerian gods as aliens is older still, expressed even in Erich von Däniken's 1968 *Chariots of the Gods?*: "Sumerian, Assyrian, Babylonian and Egyptian cuneiform inscriptions constantly present the same picture: 'gods' came from the stars and went back to them..."

But this is not the case. First, Sumerian texts are rare and spotty; they do not contain stories of the Anunnaki as such. Instead, the Anunnaki are best attested in the later Babylonian creation epic, the *Enuma Elish*, where they are simply gods created by Marduk, the chief god. He creates 600 Anunnaki, dividing them into two groups: 300 he placed in the sky, and 300 he placed in the sea down under the earth. Far from coming from the stars, in *Enuma Elish* 5.125-128, the gods in fact rise up from the underground sea called the Apsû as well as descend from the heavens:

> When you come up from the Apsû to make a decision
> This will be your resting place before the assembly.
> When you descend from heaven to make a decision
> This will be your resting place before the assembly.
>
> (trans. W. G. Lambert[4])

Thus, there is no clear implication that the gods belong to the stars.

But the Anunnaki do have an interesting role that AATs ought to have quickly embraced. In the *Enuma Elish* (6.53-63), these gods work on the earth to make bricks for Marduk's ziggurat of Esagil in Babylon, an actual building that still exists to this day:

> ["]Let us erect a shrine to house a pedestal
> Wherein we may repose when we finish (the work)."

---

[4] W. C. Lambert, "Mesopotamian Creation Stories," in M.J. Geller and M. Schipper (eds.), *Imagining Creation* (IJS Studies in Judaica 5; Brill Academic Publishers, 2007), 37-59.

When Marduk heard this,
He beamed as brightly as the light of day,
"Build Babylon, the task you have sought.
Let bricks for it be moulded, and raise the shrine!"
The Anunnaki wielded the pick.
For one year they made the needed bricks.
When the second year arrived,
They raised the peak of Esagil, a replica of the Apsû.
They built the lofty temple tower of the Apsû [...]

(trans. W. G. Lambert[5])

Reconstruction of the Etemenanki ziggurat of Babylon, 1919 drawing. (Wikimedia Commons)

Ironically, this "ancient text" actually has the Anunnaki—identified by *Ancient Aliens* as aliens—building a real, currently-extant, pyramid-shaped structure. According to the text, they built both the temple of Marduk called Esagila and the "lofty temple tower," the ziggurat of Etemenaki, that abutted it. What a shame that after archaeology failed to find extraterrestrial artifacts in any pre-

---

[5] Ibid.

historic building, modern ancient astronaut theorists no longer advocate alien construction but instead talk about more nebulous "influences."

After all, the aliens apparently didn't build to last. Ruins of Babylon, 1932. (Library of Congress)

The episode of *Ancient Aliens* claiming these Anunnaki as ETs aired September 15, 2011. Just 24 hours earlier, Giorgio Tsoukalos, TV's leading AAT, tweeted: "Repeat after me: The pyramids were NOT built by aliens. According to ancient Egyptian texts, the pyramids were built by humans WITH THE ASSISTANCE of the 'Guardians of the Sky'…"

Now the Egyptian pyramids are not the same as the Mesopotamian ziggurats, but it hardly makes sense to suggest that humans constructed the massive stone constructions of Egypt while Mesopotamia's rather simpler ziggurats, made from piles of dried mud bricks, required aliens to physically work for two years in the deserts of Iraq. Surely, if the aliens didn't build the pyramids, they did not build the ziggurats either.

Damn those lying "ancient texts"!

A problem arises in that the "ancient text" Tsoukalos cites as his source, Al-Maqrizi's *Al-Khitat*, was actually written in 1400 CE, *four thousand years* after the pyramids were built, whereas the "ancient text" telling us that the Anunnaki built the ziggurat of Babylon was written roughly at the time of the building's construction. (The ziggurat dates back perhaps as far as 1500 BCE, while the poem was first written around 1500 BCE, with surviving copies dating from 650 BCE.)

Another problem arises here. The ziggurat of Babylon, known as Etemenanki, served a secondary purpose in the Hebrew literature: Most scholars believe it was the Tower of Babel. According to AATs, however, the Tower of Babel was destroyed by aliens (pretending to be God) in order to keep humans subservient to their extraterrestrial overlords when *humans* built the tower too high. Unless they didn't. Erich von Däniken thought in *Gods from Outer Space* (1970) that the Tower of Babel was an observation post for monitoring the aliens, while Zecharia Sitchin ridiculously thought it was some kind of Saturn V-style rocket in *Twelfth Planet* (1976). This is especially ironic since Sitchin's entire corpus was predicated on the idea that the Anunnaki were aliens—and yet he misses their most significant, and testable, earthly achievement, the construction of an actual set of buildings that anyone can visit today.

Obviously, the talking heads on *Ancient Aliens* have trouble using "ancient texts" consistently, or even accurately, even when they would appear to support their own views. If the "aliens" did not build the ziggurat—and there is not a shred of evidence that anyone other than humans worked on it—then the "ancient text" cited above is wrong. And if we admit that ancient texts can be incorrect, what warrant do we have to assume they are correct about other alleged alien incidents?

EPISODE 9:
ALIENS AND DEADLY WEAPONS
September 22, 2011

EPISODE REVIEW

THIS EPISODE of *Ancient Aliens* devoted to "Aliens and Deadly Weapons"; however, at this point in the show's run—more than halfway through its third season—the deadliest weapon of all is the boring sameness of the program's many episodes. Last night's edition was no different, featuring a mixture of absurd claims unsupported by evidence, leading questions, and a few outright lies. The big news is that by this episode it appeared that some of my critiques of David Hatcher Childress's and Giorgio Tsoukalos's "evidence" must have hit home since the program contorted itself to avoid directly citing a famous and fraudulent quotation about nuclear bombs in the *Mahabharata*. But more on that anon.

The first dumb claim this hour is the idea that world mythology contains many separate tales of fire being stolen from the gods because aliens gave humans fire. No, the myth of fire from the sky most likely comes from the obvious source of the first fire—lightning. You know: that fire in the *sky*.

The ancient astronaut theorists then argue that the ancient myths attributed to blacksmiths—myths forbidding the public to gaze upon them, myths making them suspect and magical—prove they were aliens. This is not true. Blacksmiths were considered powerful and magical, but also suspect and unclean, because they could transform lumps of ore into useful weapons and tools—a process that seemed magical. If this does not seem logical to you, remember: The ancients also considered menstruation to be a mythic, magical event that rendered the menstruating woman taboo and unclean. Unless you'd like to argue that the aliens invented menstruation, there is nothing alien to read into the myths of outcast blacksmiths.

There is really no way to argue for or against claims that Hephaestus, the Japanese gods, the Archangel Michael, or other figures were actually aliens who interacted with characters like Joan of Arc. "Could Joan of Arc have been given her sword by extraterrestrials who had an interest in the future of France?" the narrator asks. Well, no. But the burden of proof here is to show this sword was made by extraterrestrials, not to disprove a wild allegation. I could very well say the sword was made by angels (as indeed Joan claimed), but to accept the reality of angels would require a bit more evidence than the testimony of an ignorant medieval peasant, or an ignorant ancient astronaut theorist.

Hephaestus married Aphrodite, so maybe there is some connection after all... Yes, that's it: Love came from aliens! (1874 illustration via Wikimedia Commons)

Next up we have King Arthur and the sword in the stone, which Giorgio Tsoukalos calls a "biometrical security system." Excalibur, Arthur's second sword, is of course an alien laser super weapon. Never mind that the story of the sword in the stone is neither unique nor original to the Arthur tale, nor are miraculous swords uncommon (they probably are related to the pagan thunder god's weapons, like Thor's hammer and Zeus's thunderbolt--symbols of lightning, not lasers). When we're making things up, we can write our own rules.

Following this, we are treated to speculation that Greek fire and gunpowder were alien inventions, the formulas bequeathed by extraterrestrials. These claims come entirely from the argument from ignorance. Just because ancient astronaut theorists don't understand how to make a chemical doesn't mean no human being ever could. Alfred Nobel managed to invent dynamite without alien help.

Arthur and Excalibur: Because the aliens keep all the really good electrical technology underwater. (1922 illustration via Wikimedia Commons)

Then we had a segment about the alleged deadly weapons of the *Mahabharata*. Unfortunately, as I have demonstrated in my earlier writings, these claims are completely false based on fabrication deriving from a purposeful rewriting and conflation of sections of the Indian epic to make them sound more like nuclear fallout. Criticism such as mine must be having some impact, however. *Ancient Aliens* at least refrained from using the completely fabricated quotation that is a standard part of ancient alien theorists' repertoire. Instead, they contorted themselves to talk *around* the false quotation, avoiding any direct citation of the *Mahabharata*. Instead, the talking heads simply asserted that the book contained tales of nuclear bombs and heat-seeking missiles, without ever citing actual passages. This is because those passages, when read in full, bear almost no resemblance to their alleged modern equivalents.

> ### Mangling the Mahabharata
>
> *"The streets swarmed with rats and mice. Earthen pots showed cracks or broke from no apparent cause. At night, the rats and mice ate away the hair and nails of slumbering men."*
>
> Mahabharata, Mausala Parva, sec. 2, Ganguli standard translation
>
> *"The corpses were so burned as to be unrecognizable. Their hair and nails fell out. Pottery broke without any apparent cause..."*
>
> The Same Passage, as given by David Childress in his *Lost Cities* series

Then it was on to Archimedes and his lasers. This is a problem, of course, because Archimedes invented a mirror to focus sunbeams *without* the help of aliens. Galienus writes in *De Temperamentis* 3.2:

> It is in this way, at least I think so, that Archimedes burnt the enemy's vessels. For, by the help of a burning mirror, he may easily set fire to wool, hemp, wood, &c.; and, in short, to any thing dry and light.
>
> (trans. in the *Edinburgh Encyclopaedia*)

Zonaras and Tzetzes confirm Galienus' account. This is neither a laser nor extraterrestrial, according to these ancient texts.

That didn't stop *Ancient Aliens*! "Ancient lasers were probably being used, and that technology probably came from extraterrestrials," said David Hatcher Childress, who in 2006 blasted me in print for claiming he was an "ancient astronaut theorist," an allegation he denied, claiming he did not believe in alien intervention. That's a laugh. Last night he continued: "Extraterrestrials may well have given man these weapons. They want us to be able to defend ourselves, to advance, and to ultimately to [sic] be like them." So, no aliens, right? Childress is an opportunistic fraud, and each appearance on *Ancient Aliens* shows how easily he transforms his "research" to match whatever "theory" will give him the most publicity.

> "[M]y whole thing is that this stuff is from this planet. These giant ruins aren't built by extraterrestrials. I say they were built by humans."
> — DAVID CHILDRESS
> *Chicago Reader*, 2006

The best way to sum up this episode is with a quotation from the lead ancient astronaut theorist: "I refuse to think our ancestors came up with these stories out of thin air," Tsoukalos said. Fine, but I refuse to believe these stories record alien intervention unless and until someone can present actual evidence of extraterrestrial presence on earth. It seems we are at an impasse. But only one of us has the burden of proving aliens were really here. I'll wait with baited breath for any real evidence.

EPISODE 3:
ALIENS AND SACRED PLACES
AUGUST 11, 2011

EPISODE 10:
ALIENS AND EVIL PLACES
SEPTEMBER 28, 2011

EPISODE REVIEW

AT THIS POINT in the run of *Ancient Aliens*, more than halfway through its third season, it has become clear that the producers never expected the series to last this long. Where the early episodes of seasons one and two moved quickly and covered the "classic" ancient "mysteries" of the ancient astronaut theory, more recent episodes have slowed the pace considerably and spent increasing time talking to people other than ancient astronaut theorists. This seems to be a confession on the part of Prometheus Entertainment that they are running out of material.

How else to explain this embarrassing hour of television called "Aliens and Evil Places," which even by the low standards of cable mystery-mongering failed the first function of television: to entertain? Since the production was so lazy, I found it difficult to muster up the energy to watch it again to pull out quotations. I decided to just wing it. Heaven knows they did.

The premise of "Aliens and Evil Places" is that some places around the world "feel" charged with evil energy, and this evil energy comes from the long ago presence of extraterrestrials (or as Giorgio Tsoukalos puts it, "*extra*terres*t*rials"), preserved in folk memory as frightening, scary creatures. Or maybe it has to do with alien uranium mines, or alien missile defense shields. One of those, definitely. But mostly the "feeling" part.

Now, it wasn't that long ago that this season's third episode of *Ancient Aliens*, "Aliens and Sacred Places," claimed that alien visitation made places sacred, so it is somewhat disconcerting to see the same "experts" argue with equal vehemence that ancient people thought aliens (whom, we must remember, they are supposed to have viewed as "gods") made places "evil." The apparent explanation is the un-evidenced supposition that there are multiple groups of aliens, some good and some evil, and usually at war. To put this in even geekier terms, this is something like discussing the battles of the war between the Green Lanterns and the Sinestro Corps without bothering to establish whether Green Lanterns exist (they don't).

But no matter. Because the criteria for judging an alien presence has been downgraded from physical evidence or even textual evidence to merely a "feeling" that a place is "creepy" or "evil," ancient astronaut theorists are now free to see aliens everywhere without fear of having their alleged evidence actually examined. How can one argue with a feeling?

Of course, if a creepy feeling is all it takes to prove aliens were involved, then nearly every town in America must be infested with extraterrestrials.

The Ghost House at Fort George Island, Fla. in 1886, an eerie ruin believed to be haunted. If the ancient astronaut theory is true, such eerie ruins mark the spots where aliens spent the night, like those inns that claim Washington slept there. (Library of Congress)

Every town has a house like the one above, an abandoned old place usually known as a "ghost house" or a "witch house," the alleged site of eerie events. Such houses are found everywhere, and

> "To the sublime in building, greatness of dimension seems requisite; for on a few parts, and those small, the imagination cannot rise to any idea of infinity. No greatness in the manner can effectually compensate for the want of proper dimensions."
>
> EDMUND BURKE, *On the Sublime and Beautiful* (1756)

they certainly cannot all be built on the sites of alien encounters. Instead, the answer is to be found in Edmund Burke's 1756 treatise *On the Sublime and Beautiful*, where he argued that large, imposing ruins and dark, eerie nights are elements that induce a feeling of the sublime. In other words, sites have stories attached to them because they make us feel a connection to the sublime; they do not become sublime through the stories circulating around them. This is the feeling that the ignorant "experts" on *Ancient Aliens* tried and failed to describe, for they had not the words to express a philosophical concept at odds with the dull literalism of the ancient astronaut theory.

Finally, the whopper of the week: In discussing Australian aboriginal mythology, the narrator of *Ancient Aliens* asked whether the "rainbow serpent," a flying Aboriginal mythic figure, was in fact an alien spaceship. A clue to why this is not true can be found in the name of the creature.

The rainbow serpent is actually believed to live *underground*, not in the sky. He can be found primarily in waterholes and the name derives from the rainbow formed when sunlight strikes the water, making little ripples that look like the body of a Technicolor serpent moving beneath the surface. This serpent is a creature of deep water, not deep space, and is obviously immensely different from flying saucers, rocket ships, and other things that streak across the daytime sky.

Ok, so that's a rainbow in the sky. That means the arc in the water is... wait.... yes... an alien spaceship! (Image: Commander John Bortniak, NOAA Corps)

Of course, if we seriously hold that Aboriginal people cannot distinguish between a rainbow in a puddle and a flying saucer in the sky, then quite clearly the famous internet meme Nyan Cat is also a symbol of ancient aliens. Think about it: The cat bears an uncanny resemblance to the "Grey" species of alien. His pop tart body is quite clearly an ignorant artist's attempt to depict a flying saucer, while the rainbow emerging from behind Nyan Cat (flying through *space* no less!) clearly represents the light trail burned into the eyes of those who dare stare at the quick-darting brilliance of the extraterrestrial feline traveler. On what grounds can we deny that Nyan Cat is clear and unambiguous evidence of extraterrestrial intervention in cyberspace?

EPISODE 11:
ALIENS AND THE FOUNDING FATHERS
OCTOBER 5, 2011

EPISODE REVIEW

THE WEEK THIS EPISODE AIRED, there was a death in my family, so I was less than enthusiastic about reviewing *Ancient Aliens*' ridiculous claims, including the use of at least two known hoaxes as "evidence." This episode, "Aliens and the Founding Fathers," spent an hour suggesting that America's founders were the recipients of extraterrestrial wisdom. But it was telling that most of the talking heads were not ancient astronaut theorists (AATs), and it was mostly left to the voiceover narration to launch into speculation about George Washington et al.'s alien encounters.

The majority of the episode featured warmed-over conspiracy theories about the Freemasons, long debunked, and occult theorizing about the Masonic symbolism of Washington, D.C.'s architecture leftover from other, sturdier History Channel programs. As the "experts" interviewed on *Ancient Aliens* strained to force E.T. into their prefabricated conspiracies—one talking head actually said that one could call a "heavenly being" seen by George Washington an extraterrestrial but it was a "heavenly being"—it was quite obvious that the program existed primarily as thematic lead-in and cross-promotional opportunity for *Brad Meltzer's Decoded*, then airing immediately after *Ancient Aliens* and which does cryptographic fantasies much better. As with *Ancient Aliens*' earlier episode devoted to promoting the movie *Cowboys & Aliens*, an alleged "truth" came a distant second to the commercial necessities of corporate synergy.

The main lines of "evidence" were laughably bad—not to mention fraudulent. One piece of evidence was an alleged vision George Washington had of a "heavenly being" that showed him "the birth, progress, and destiny of the Republic of the United States" while at

Valley Forge. AAT Giorgio Tsoukalos and *Ancient Aliens* took this as a genuine vision (albeit of an "alien" and not an angel) reported by the 99-year-old Anthony Sherman, a (non-existent) former aid to Washington, in 1859, as told to Wesley Bradshaw. In fact, this is a well-known hoax concocted by Charles W. Alexander, the actual author of the piece, in 1861, at the start of the Civil War. It was intended as fiction, hence the anachronistic references to the "Union" projected back to 1777-1778. Another claim made by *Ancient Aliens*, that Washington was visited by "Greenskins," or alien beings, derives entirely from hoax diaries allegedly found in a Scottish castle in the 1990s and later reported on by a British tabloid reporter in the *Sun*. As far as I can tell, such diaries have never been published and in all likelihood do not exist.

After seeing credence given to a hoax exposed at least as early as 1917 and another with no supporting evidence whatsoever, what purpose is there in bothering to examine the AATs' other "evidence"?

Whopper of the week: The dumbest claim has to be that the streets of Washington, D.C. were laid out in the shape of a five-pointed star to communicate to the aliens that we "respect" them. Do I even have to mention that real stars do not have points, and the convention of five points on a star would have no relevance whatsoever to beings unfamiliar with the convention? Heck, even in Western civilization we don't always use five points on a star. Sometimes we have four (like many depictions of the star of Bethlehem), six (the asterisk—literally, star), or seven (a sheriff's badge).

EPISODE 12:
ALIENS AND DEADLY CULTS
OCTOBER 12, 2011

EPISODE REVIEW

> "Do alien visitors really desire the blood of humans in order to exert power and gain control over the earth?"
>
> NARRATION, *Ancient Aliens*, "Aliens and Deadly Cults"

FUNNY, I thought that was vampires.

This *Ancient Aliens* episode used its conceit as an excuse to rehash the most salacious aspects of ancient and modern cults, including the Thugees of India and Heaven's Gate. Mostly the show talked about human sacrifice, murder, castration, mass suicide, etc. and then threw in random moments of ancient astronaut theorists (AATs) claiming that the gods worshipped by the cults were actually aliens. But this is largely irrelevant, since the cults were comprised of human beings, and the aliens or the gods never showed up. Later, when the show said AATs believe that aliens were really in touch with modern cult leaders like Marshall Herff Applewhite of Heaven's Gate through brain implants and ordered them to commit mass suicide, the show crossed the line from irresponsible to perverse.

Much hay is made of the so-called "Brotherhood of the Snake," a supposedly ancient secret society founded by extraterrestrials but perverted into a sinister force. The AATs attribute evidence of this society to unnamed "ancient legends," but so far as I can tell the first mention of this supposed secret society didn't come until the twentieth century, when William Bramley described them in 1989's *The Gods of Eden*, which drew its "knowledge" of Mesopotamian (Sumerian and Babylonian) mythology from Zecharia Sitchin's eccentric interpretations.

> "Surely Jesus of Nazareth would have hardly advised his apostles to show themselves as wise *as the serpent,* had the latter been a symbol of the Evil one; *nor would the Ophites, the learned Egyptian Gnostics of "the Brotherhood of the Serpent," have reverenced a living snake in their ceremonies as the emblem of* **WISDOM***, the divine Sophia (and a type of the all-good, not the all-bad), were that reptile so closely connected with Satan."*
>
> HELENA BLAVATSKY, *The Secret Doctrine*

The closest pre-Bramley source appears to be the Ophites (from the Greek for "snake"), a Gnostic group who had taken the snake as their symbol, and were referred to as the Brotherhood of the Serpent in Blavatsky's *Secret Doctrine* (1888) and *only* in Blavatsky and those dependent upon her. Peter Tompkins says that a "Brotherhood of the Serpent" among the Maya were extraterrestrials in his 1987 *Mysteries of the Mexican Pyramids*. There was also a "brotherhood of the Snake" mentioned in a 1929 *Journal of American Folklore* article, but this refers to a Native American group within one southwestern tribe. Another, fictional, Brotherhood of the Snake occurred in the 1916 novel *The Boy Settler* by Edwin Legrand Sabin.

Bramley does not provide "ancient legends" of the "Brotherhood" in his book. Instead, he conjures the existence of the Brotherhood out of two parts: First, world mythologies feature frequent allusions to serpent worship, which he takes a unified cult symbol. Second, he then imagines that the Sumerian gods are flesh-and-blood extraterrestrials, meaning that Sumerian myths are minutes taken at the meetings of the

Brotherhood, whose members masqueraded as gods. But look at how Bramley first introduces his Brotherhood:

> The snake was the logo of a group which had become very influential in early human societies of both Hemispheres. That group was a disciplined Brotherhood dedicated to the dissemination of spiritual knowledge and the attainment of spiritual freedom. This Brotherhood of the Snake (also known as the 'Brotherhood of the Serpent,' but which I will often refer to as simply the "Brotherhood") opposed the enslavement of spiritual beings and, according to Egyptian writings, it sought to liberate the human race from Custodial bondage. The Brotherhood also imparted scientific knowledge and encouraged the high aesthetics that existed in many ancient societies. For these and other reasons, the snake had become a venerated symbol to humans and, according to Egyptian and biblical texts, an object of Custodial hatred.
>
> (1990 paperback ed., pp. 53-4)

Note that there is no evidence whatsoever presented for the group's existence. The group is presented as an assertion in the first sentence, given a name without a source in the third, and *only then* is evidence marshaled to support the supposition—but this evidence, the Bible and Egyptian texts, says nothing about any brotherhood of the snake. Instead, these are mere mentions of snakes that Bramley *has chosen to interpret as evidence of a unified snake cult*. In other words, this is nothing but circular reasoning.

For whatever reason, once Bramley proposed the Snake Brotherhood, other authors picked up on it, dozens in the five years following publication of the *Gods of Eden*. In 1993 Jan van Helsing discussed the cult as having been formed in early Mesopotamia c. 300,000 BCE. Van Helsing's name is a pseudonym, chosen in honor of the famous vampire hunter, because Jan van Helsing believed

Jews were bloodsuckers who used the Brotherhood of the Snake to control the world. This was one of the more disturbing uses of Bramley's imaginary brotherhood.

The cult was popularized by David Icke in 1999's *The Biggest Secret*, and, unfortunately, through *Ancient Aliens*, which let Bramley assert without foundation that his circular reasoning had some basis in fact outside of his own head.

But that describes all of *Ancient Aliens*—random facts marshaled with circular logic into self-referential "theories."

EPISODE 13:
ALIENS AND THE SECRET CODE
OCTOBER 19, 2011

EPISODE REVIEW

IN THIS EPISODE, the producers of *Ancient Aliens* proposed that the "extraterrestrials" left a "secret code" in the form of prehistoric sites scattered across the world, built (depending on which segment one watched) according to UFO flight paths, magnetic lay lines, geodesy, or an "energy grid."

I can't begin to describe the stupidity of the idea that this imaginary "energy grid" (which has not been proven to exist) let ancient people move large rocks to build ancient structures through conveniently lost anti-gravity devices (based on "free and inexhaustible energy," David Hatcher Childress asserts). What type of "energy" this is, I can't imagine; the ancient astronaut theorists (AATs) elide magnetic fields, gravitational fields, and various mystic energy forms all under the unscientific ideas of "energy." Apparently, every ancient civilization listened to ancient astronauts, who told them to build temples on sites where this "energy grid" had power points. These were airports, or something like that, for "refueling" UFOs.

Of course, the supposed precision of the show's map of this grid is completely fictitious, based entirely on selecting ancient sites to match its supposed nodes while ignoring those that do not match. Many popular "node" maps place Machu Picchu (or Cuzco) and the Great Pyramid on nodes, but few of them include such ancient sites as the ziggurat of Ur, the Lascaux caves, the great mound of Cahokia, Teotihuacan, the most ancient mud-brick cities of Peru, etc. Logically, one would expect the oldest sites, like those of Sumer or pre-Inca Peru (coeval with the Great Pyramid, after all), to have a place in the node system. I would love to give a more thorough discussion, but as it turns out, no two "researchers" agree where these energy nodes are, making it impossible to develop criteria to evaluate ancient sites' correspondence to them. Nevertheless, all agree the "nodes" are a secret code.

A major problem with the idea that ancient cultures developed a secret "code" to signal knowledge of the aliens for future generations is the idea that ancient cultures had a conception of time that allowed for an understanding that their cultures would die, and that others would supersede them. Most ancient cultures for which we have evidence believed they could trace their origins back to the creation of the world (see Genesis or the *Enuma Elish*, for instance); therefore, their traditions and their culture were primeval and, for all intents and purposes, eternal. Any culture that believed its origins were coeval with creation could hardly be accused of planning for its own destruction.

Many ancient cultures believed in some form of cyclical time, best represented by the Hindu concept of world ages. Accordingly, the ancients as a general rule imagined that their culture would continue on until the world age ended, time restarted, and the world began anew. In such a situation, there is no reason to plan for imaginary future cultures, which would be serviced by the new generation of gods, or to signal them about knowledge of the former world that they would not need and could not use.

The rest of the episode's claims—about ley lines as memories of UFO flight paths, about ancient temples as UFO refueling stations, etc.—are all predicated on fictitious knowledge of how alien spacecraft would operate (assumptions about their fuel, flight plans, etc.) drawn from analogies with contemporary airplanes and airports—not likely to be truly analogous to craft from another world, operating under another set of technologies and assumptions. AATs' claims that the ancients had super-advanced math skills are belied by the fact that the Greeks were happy to say π was $^{22}/_7$ and took a thousand years to invent the Pythagorean theorem, or that 0 didn't manage to make headway outside India. Have you ever tried doing calculus with Roman numerals? It doesn't really work.

A segment on Cuzco's role as a "world navel" is just stupid because Cuzco wasn't constructed until c. 1000 CE (by the Killke culture) or inhabited by the Inca until the thirteenth century CE. This is not very ancient. In that same period, Charlemagne had come and gone in Europe, Mayan civilization had collapsed, and the Arab world was at the height of its scientific prowess. Had the aliens come and established a world navel then, surely someone would have recorded some unambiguous evidence of their existence—or, better, would not some physical evidence still remain? After all, archaeologists have recently discovered actual loaves of bread baked in those years, but not a single piece of extraterrestrial technology.

Similarly, the idea that ancient monuments like the Jerusalem Temple (the site where the Dome of the Rock now stands) were built atop stone slabs used for docking spaceships is just silly. Why did spacecraft need stone platforms to take off and land? Does this not beg us to ask how the first ships managed to land so the aliens could enslave the populace to build their giant stone landing pads?

The essential problem is this: *Ancient Aliens* elides all of history—from the earliest Paleolithic cultures to dynastic Egypt to the Bronze Age to the Middle Ages—under the rubric of "ancient" and imagines that there was a unified program extending across time and space, among unrelated cultures, for anywhere from 5,000 to 15,000 years. And all of this simply vanished without even a scrap of incontrovertible physical evidence of interaction between far-flung cultures or contact with extraterrestrials, conveniently just at the time when those evil "scientists" began investigating the world in the early modern period.

With only three more *Ancient Aliens* episodes left in the third season, I looked with trepidation toward the following week's Halloween special on the "Undead." Horror monsters are my area of expertise, and I did not think I'd be too happy to hear AATs claim that vampires and zombies were the result of extraterrestrial intervention. Fortunately for me, it turned out that the promotional spots for the episode were every bit as much a fraud as the theories AATs advocate.

EPISODE 14:
ALIENS AND THE UNDEAD
October 26, 2011

EPISODE REVIEW

Ancient Aliens tried to claim that the undead were not "mere myths" but really extraterrestrials in the episode "Aliens and the Undead." Sadly, however, the first half hour did not focus on vampires and zombies as promised but instead went the more prosaic route of exploring whether Egyptian mummies had a relationship to alien cryogenic body preservation technology, and whether afterlife deities were actually extraterrestrials.

Much hay was made from the odd, elongated shape of the depiction of the heads of the Egyptian pharaoh Akhenaton and his family, arguing that this was an imitation of alien skulls. Similar skulls, the program notes, are found in Peru, but such deformations are rather easy to produce with infant head-binding. There is no particular reason to imagine a connection between Egypt and Peru, much less an extraterrestrial one. While the program claims "only" the alien-influenced cultures of Peru and Egypt practiced cranial deformation, in fact Neanderthals did it 45,000 years ago, as did early human cultures of the Neolithic and historically-documented groups in Australia, the Pacific Islands, North America, and late Antique Europe (the Huns and Alans, and the Germanic peoples they influenced). So, chalk one up to another flat-out *Ancient Aliens* lie. (We will discuss this again in Season 4 Episode 3, "The Greys," when the show contradicts this episode's claims.)

Then, halfway through, we finally got to the vampires. But of course *Ancient Aliens* managed to muck it up by conflating vampires with vengeful spirits and blood-sucking demons and then calling all of them "extraterrestrials abandoned here on earth." Because aliens apparently like to suck blood ("cosmic fuel," the narrator said) since, you know, creatures from another world clearly have evolved to survive on the blood of mammals. (Funny, I thought the aliens ate gold, as per Laurence Gardner, building on Zecharia Sitchin.) But no! Minutes later it isn't that aliens are eating the blood. Instead, the "theory" is now that human blood loss leads to altered states of consciousness that open human minds to extraterrestrial worlds through some kind of quantum window. Or, as David Hatcher Childress claims, ritual bloodletting, as in Mayan rituals, is merely the aliens' way of showing us "how important" our blood is. As opposed, apparently, to spinal fluid or various internal organs.

The program wonders what it takes to bring a dead person back to life (other than, of course, CPR, or, today, a defibrillator). Childress, stupidly, states: "What kind of powers would you have to have to do that? The powers of an extraterrestrial?" No, just a lifeguard. Remember, this man spent the last three decades vehemently arguing that he was not an ancient astronaut theorist. Now he talks of how the aliens will shepherd our souls to the stars after death.

Ancient Aliens speculates that the "aliens" exist on a separate plane from us and our souls will move to that space after death, where we will rejoin the aliens in a cosmic paradise. At some point these aliens stopped having any meaningful distinction from the gods they were originally proposed to replace. At this point, we might as well give up the concept of "ancient aliens" altogether and admit that the ancient astronaut theorists just want the pagan gods to be real so they can give them magic gifts.

EPISODE 15:
ALIENS, GODS, AND HEROES
NOVEMBER 16, 2011

EPISODE REVIEW

ANCIENT ASTRONAUT THEORISTS (AATs) have a problem distinguishing fact from fantasy. But that's a given. In this episode of *Ancient Aliens*, "Aliens Gods, and Heroes," the program attempts to make hay from the fact that the site on Crete traditionally associated with the birth of Zeus contains Minoan-era religious artifacts. This, supposedly, is amazing proof that Greek myths record real alien encounters. It does not cross the minds of the ancient alien theorists that the cave became associated with the Greek gods *because* it had been a sacred site under the preceding Mycenaean and Minoan civilizations. This is not dissimilar to the way early Christian churches were built atop pagan temples. The site was already holy, and it remained so even as ideologies and faiths changed.

It is also ridiculous that people who supposedly understand mythology are completely unaware of the mutual influences between mythologies. The similarities between Greek, Hittite, and Babylonian stories of the succession of the gods (the overthrow of early deities by younger gods—as Zeus overthrew Kronos who overthrew Ouranos, for example) are due not to these various cultures recording alien spaceships in dogfights but because (big shock here) Mesopotamian myths spread outward to the Hittites and eventually the Greeks. The stories are the same because—again, big shock—they are the *same story*.

We then rehash the same material about whether aliens created humanity, once more showing the ancient astronaut theory's real, underlying purpose—to resurrect the authority of ancient religious traditions by wrapping them in the borrowed finery of science. Ancient astronaut theorists will deny it, but they, like Creationists, ultimately want to undo Darwin's revolution by marrying religion to a bastardized form of science.

Oh, and *Ancient Astronauts* also wants to relate all of this to comic books because, you know, *Captain America* and *Green Lantern* were totally things back when they filmed the show during the summer of 2011.

I won't dignify Giorgio Tsoukalos' dumb claim that "ancient texts" prove invisibility technology is real because Greek figures like Perseus and various Hindu figures have invisibility helmets, cloaks, etc. It's one of the oldest folkloric tropes, but if we follow Tsoukalos' reckoning, then Ambrose Bierce's "Damned Thing" would prove that *Predator* was a documentary. Heck, while I'm on the subject, I edited an entire anthology of short stories about invisible monsters called *Unseen Horror* (2011). Imagining invisibility is not exactly rocket science, to coin a phrase.

Also, Tsoukalos, amazed that some pre-Columbian rituals are still performed today, finds it astonishing that ancient mythology is performed "before our very eyes." Apparently he's never been to a church, or a Native American ceremony, or a Buddhist service. Specifically, he complained that the *voladores,* Mexican performers who swing down on ropes from a tower in honor of the gods, were misunderstood. "Where does that flying or descending gods motif originate? Our ancestors saw something…" This couldn't have anything to do with birds or the sky. "Birds are not that important. Something significant happened." Not to burst his bubble, but neither birds nor aliens underlies myths of sky gods. Neuroscience shows that the human brain evolved to conceive of three planes—the underworld, the earth, and the heavens. The gods live in the sky because that is where our brains instinctively place them. The scholar David Lewis-Williams did much work in this area in *The Mind in the Cave* (2002) and its sequel. This, Lewis-Williams would argue, is the true origin of sky gods and the quest for flight—not aliens.

Then, for no good reason, we move on to the ocean. Why? Because this episode seems to be made up of leftover parts that didn't fit anywhere else. The program evinces no real understanding that the classical Greek god Poseidon derived from an earlier Mycenaean god of earthquakes, *Po-se-da-wo-ne*, who cannot be proved (from extant Linear B texts and archaeological remains) to have been associated with the sea at that early date. Indo-European theorists suggest Poseidon derives in part from a god of springs and fresh water, only later applied to the sea when the Indo-Europeans migrated to Greece.

All of which is much more interesting than the claim that Kronos vomiting up his children really derives from aliens escaping an exploding mother-ship and taking their escape pods to earth. And then they had sex with people—which is weird since the first half hour argued that the gods were already living here when they "created" people. Oh, well. Consistency is for uptight elitists. The children of these unions were apparently memories of ancient scuba gear. Whatever. Let's try proving these wonder kids exist before we speculate on the size of their oxygen tanks.

All of these dumb claims are predicated on the idea that there is one universally recognized, true Greek mythology. But there isn't. The early myths preserved in Homer and Hesiod (700-600 BCE) differ wildly from their final decayed form in Nonnus' *Dionysiaca* (c. 400 CE). The versions given in the handbooks of Thomas Bulfinch, Edith Hamilton, and H. J. Rose are "standard" only in that they are the versions that modern people have come to accept as "correct." They are not the only versions of these stories—and in many cases not the versions that the ancients of Hesiod's day would recognize, and certainly not anyone before Hesiod. To base wild theories on Greek myths requires an understanding of how they grew and changed over time. But that takes real work and real thought and a real engagement with primary sources, and we all know ancient astronaut theorists will never do that.

EPISODE 16:
ALIENS AND THE CREATION OF MAN
NOVEMBER 23, 2011

EPISODE REVIEW

THIS EPISODE aired just before Thanksgiving in the United States, and I for one knew what I was thankful for that day: This was the final episode of *Ancient Aliens* for 2011. Yes, indeed, I could look forward to at least a couple of months without any new ridiculousness about alien artists, warriors, and genetic engineers. On his Twitter feed, lead ancient astronaut theorist (AAT) Giorgio Tsoukalos billed this season finale as the "best ever" episode and one that was something called "Tsoukalicious," but I'm just glad it's over.

As a personal note, I had a terrible headache that day and could barely force myself to watch *Ancient Aliens*, made worse by History's decision to show the program's HD finale in the wrong aspect ratio, squishing the images down into a thin strip across the middle of the screen and making everyone look wide and weird.

But these were technical problems. The episode itself, "Aliens and the Creation of Man," has inherent in its title a revealing correspondence between the ancient astronaut theory and religious-oriented creationism (also: sexism—women exist, too). In both cases, the modern theory of evolution is suspect, and the existence of human beings is attributed to a higher power for a greater purpose. And in both cases, the trappings of science are misused to give the alternative theory a spurious credibility, implicitly conceding that in the modern world science is the arbiter of truth. As with creationism, the ancient astronaut theory is an attempt to preserve the power of traditional religious text and cultural heritage by giving it a (false) scientific respectability on which to base a literal understanding of ancient texts.

Tsoukalos knows nothing about evolution. He complains that humans could not have lost their body hair early on as the result of evolutionary change because humans immediately began wearing furs to survive winter. Having rejected evolution, I suppose it means nothing to him that humans evolved in sub-Saharan Africa, where snowy winters do not exist, and during a period when the earth was warmer than in the succeeding Ice Age. Then David Childress (he dropped the Hatcher apparently) trots out old Victorian spiritualist speculation as "proof" that "scientists" reject atheistic evolution. Whatever. Victorians also believed in phlogiston, vampires, man-eating jungle plants, and fairies. They are not unimpeachable authorities.

The human brain is next celebrated as a masterpiece of invention, and therefore a genetic legacy of aliens rather than evolution. (Ok, so where did the aliens come from?) Apparently the aliens were lonely and wanted creatures who could communicate through language. Dolphins have rudimentary language, so I guess the aliens were just messing with them for fun.

But then George Noory of *Coast to Coast AM* claimed Adam and Eve was a "true story" despite the clear evidence that the tale is much later than its Sumerian original—an original that lacks the details found in Genesis. Childress chimes in about the reality of the Tree of Knowledge. Tsoukalos then offers his view of Satan, that he was a rebel alien (something like Scientology's mythology, I guess). Of course he is wildly ignorant of the true origins of the Christian devil figure in a conflation of the Hebrew accuser (an agent of God in Job, for example) and a misreading of select passages about other figures (like Isaiah's discussion of Nebuchadnezzar, which Christians reinterpreted as the fall of Lucifer, misreading figurative language

> "How art thou fallen from heaven, O Lucifer, son of the morning! how art thou cut down to the ground, which didst weaken the nations!"
>
> ISAIAH 14:12

about the king as "morning star" (*Lucifer,* or light-bringer, in the Latin of the Vulgate) as an angel named Light Bringer, or Lucifer (Isaiah 14).

The problem, of course, is that Biblical literalism is wrong no matter what idea it supports. To imagine biblical texts as literally true is to ignore the vast evidence that these texts have been altered and adapted over time. Even Isaiah 14, referring to Nebuchadnezzar, probably originates in a still earlier poem written for a different subject. The point is that taking ancient texts at face value is sloppy scholarship.

No time for such thoughts, however, since we are next off to Mesopotamia to belatedly acknowledge that the Biblical texts are predated by Sumerian, Assyrian, and Babylonian myths—though there is no acknowledgement that the Biblical texts were influenced by these older models, only that there is an "echo" from various cultures all discussing the same aliens. Instead, we are treated to warmed-over Zecharia Sitchin, with various talking heads claiming (falsely) that the Mesopotamian creation myth plainly tells that the gods created humans to mine gold to power the aliens' planet. It does not. This is what the *Enuma Elish* says (Marduk is speaking):

> I will solidify blood, I will form bone.
> I will set up man, 'Man' [shall be] his name.
> I will create the man 'Man.'
> The service of the gods shall be established, and I will set them
>   (i.e., the gods) free.
>
> (6.3-6, trans. E. A. Wallis Budge)

So, not gold mining but worship of the gods was the reason for the creation of man, for the gods had, a few lines earlier, complained that their existence was futile without worship. (The gods were tired of building temples with their own hands, so the servant angle is right, just not the gold mining to fuel rogue planets part.)

Then we're off to the panspermia theory, suggesting comets brought life to earth from alien worlds when microbes hitched a ride on comets. This, of course, directly contradicts everything the ancient astronaut theory stands for (since no actual intelligent aliens are visiting earth) but you know what they say about consistency and mediocre minds. I suppose one could suggest that the comets were seeded by aliens to terraform other planets like ours, but I'd think that a billion years is a long time to wait for the garden to grow.[6] But since AATs don't believe in evolution, they don't have to worry about the likelihood that any aliens terraforming worlds a billion years ago either evolved beyond recognition or went extinct eons ago. They could not be the gods in flying saucers from the first fifty minutes of the program.

The grand finale is the assertion that extraterrestrials in no way disprove God but instead form a middle layer between God and humanity (i.e., angels). Thus, the program's talking heads prove the point I made a few hundred words ago, that ancient astronaut theories are simply creationism by other means, an attempt to hold on to religion in the face of science.

And we're done with Season Three! Free! Free at last! Or at least until Season Four. God (or Xenu or whatever) help us all.

---

[6] Ridley Scott disagreed and based his movie *Prometheus* (2012) on just such an ancient astronaut theory.

ANCIENT ALIENS
SEASON FOUR

EPISODE 1:
THE MAYAN CONSPIRACY
February 17, 2012

EPISODE REVIEW

JUDGING FROM MY EMAIL, it seems that a sizable part of the audience for *Ancient Aliens* felt that there was a conspiracy to suppress the program when History moved the show to sister station H2 at the beginning of Season Four. It was so well hidden in fact that the conspiracy had History simulcast the first episode on its main channel, just to make sure no one saw it.

The first episode of *Ancient Aliens*' new season asked whether the Maya were influenced by aliens. Most of the episode's territory had been explored in Alan Landsburg's *The Outer Space Connection* (1975), right down to the claim that the Maya expected the aliens to return when the stars came right again. But unlike Landsburg, *Ancient Aliens* left out the cryogenically frozen clones that the aliens were supposed to come back for. This is an improvement of sorts.

One thing that immediately struck me is that the episode had many more real scholars in it than previous outings, probably because they needed people who actually know real things about the Maya in order to explain the culture, since clearly ancient astronaut theorists know nothing about the Maya except what they have read in secondhand sources. Plus, there are only so many times you can say "aliens did it" without becoming repetitive. Many scholars I've talked with have mixed feelings about appearing on shows like *Ancient Aliens*, and the presence of real archaeologists offers a false equivalency that ends up making ancient astronaut theorists (AATs) look more reasonable and credible than they are.

Before we get into the meat of the episode, there is an important fact about the Maya that we have to keep in mind, and one that *Ancient Aliens* did its best to hide. The program discusses Mayan pyramids, texts, and carvings *as they exist today*, representing the last years of Maya culture. This was not in some remote period of prehistory. These ruins represent the Classic and Post-Classic periods, roughly contemporary with late Antique and early medieval Europe. The Classic Period runs from 200-1000 CE, but *Ancient Aliens* treats the Maya as though their culture emerged fully formed, with no understanding of the formative Paleo-Indian and Archaic and Pre-Classic periods that preceded the Classic. When, exactly, did the aliens arrive? In the Classic? Well, "alien" pyramids began long before then. The Pre-Classic? If so, then did they come back again in the Classic, say at Palenque between 603 and 638 CE, when AATs claim Lord Pacal rode to space in a rocket ship?

This is the equivalent of arguing that Justinian's church of Hagia Sophia (built 527-537 CE) is an alien monument since it is a large, sophisticated building in a mysterious and complex culture, while ignoring the existence of Greece and Rome before it. But who'd buy that Byzantine culture came from aliens?

Now that we have our chronology straight, it's time to get into the episode proper.

It Really Isn't Rocket Science

Near the beginning, journalist Philip Coppens declared the Maya the "most advanced" ancient civilization, which is patently ridiculous since these people had not invented the arch, made use of wheels, or took advantage of any of the many advances enjoyed by contemporary peoples. Also, as noted, they weren't really that ancient, unless you consider Charlemagne ancient. The Classic Maya, remember, were contemporaneous with the Romans and Byzantines, who had arches and concrete and seagoing ships and a vast imperial infrastructure. The Maya had none of this.

But all this Maya madness is territory well-trod since at least von Däniken's dumb idea about Lord Pacal's tomb depicting a man in a rocket (a very small rocket, apparently). Naturally, the tomb lid appears here as most important piece of evidence in the ancient astronaut theory. David Childress (apparently definitively dropping the "Hatcher" and once more becoming an ancient astronaut theorist) credited Lord Pacal as "the original rocket man," which was neither clever nor accurate. Giorgio Tsoukalos noted Pacal was in the position used by modern day astronauts for lift off, which is of course as conclusive as it comes.

A modeler made a 3-D imaginary version of Pacal's tomb as a space ship, and Tsoukalos declared that the model "is a dream come true." Neither seemed aware that applying one's own bias to creating the model produces not evidence but a circular argument, where the premises ("this is a rocket") yield the conclusion ("this is a rocket"). The most important confession comes when the modeler explains he had to "interpret" the plaque and add things that weren't there (thrusters) to make it more like a rocket. "Of course!" Tsoukalos declares. Now, think about this: A capsule less than six feet tall is attached to "thrusters"

> *"It was a bizarre scene, though von Däniken's explanation didn't quite make sense to me. The man was barefoot and wore no shirt, a typical dress for the Maya, but is this how one dresses when one is in one's space ship? ... it is unlikely that any sort of rocket power was ever used in the past or will ever be used in the future by visiting astronauts ..."*
>
> DAVID CHILDRESS on Pacal's tomb in 1992's *Lost Cities of North and Central America*

that are supposed to send it safely to escape velocity with no apparent fuel tanks. The stupid thing would explode at ignition. Of course, you could argue it used sophisticated technology, but if so, it shouldn't have all the smoke and flame AATs imagine are visible in Pacal's tomb lid.

Turning to other Maya sculptures, Tsoukalos sees cockpits and rockets everywhere, interpreting geometric shapes as *prima facie* evidence for high technology, since technology has geometric shapes. But then so too does math homework, so maybe that's what it was after all.

Flying African Alien Astronauts?

Ah, but the Maya aren't enough to fill an hour on their own, so we next switch to the Olmec of thousands of years earlier, with weird claims that their colossal stone heads are "maybe aliens" because their headgear looks like space helmets. Childress and Tsoukalos, ignorant of everything, claim that Olmec sculptures depict Africans, apparently unaware of actual native peoples of the region who closely resemble the Olmec sculptures found there. Tsoukalos believes one statue in particular depicts an African wearing a space suit with wings to fly from Africa to Mexico to spread the aliens' message. This is yet another case where you see what you want to see when looking at the statue. All I see is a king or priest in his ceremonial outfit, draped in necklaces and pectorals and other jewelry. Besides, how can the aliens have needed space suits if they also had sex with humans, as ancient astronaut theorists claim? (The "visitors had sexual intercourse with our ancestors," von Däniken told *Playboy* in 1974.) And why would Africans need "life support" on earth?

Oh, well, enough Olmecs. Now we're back to the Maya, this time at Copan, abandoned in the ninth century CE. Surprisingly, much of this segment relies on real archaeologists discussing the actual content of Mayan hieroglyphs, with their emphasis on recording the lineage and deeds of the kings. But then someone who can't read the hieroglyphs, Giorgio Tsoukalos, claims that the Maya priests who wrote them were in contact with aliens they mistook for gods and used their alien power as "a way to keep the common people in place." Interestingly, this is what AATs think about scientists today, an elite trying to suppress the truth about aliens and keep the common people ignorant. Coincidence?

The Blood Is the Life

Childress mentions that the Mayan gods "came from the sky," as though this were proof of alien origins. But this is simplistic. Not all the gods came from the sky. The Mayan death gods, for example, are chthonic deities, who live in Xibalba under the earth. This is not the same as the sky. But the Maya apparently wanted their alien overlords to return, and they sacrificed each other willy-nilly to get the aliens (who must be vampires) to come back.

"Blood sacrifice was nothing else but an act of desperation to bring about the return of the extraterrestrials," Tsoukalos said, arguing that every culture has a promised return of the gods. This is *false*. The Greek gods never promised "to return," for they never left. The Sumerian gods will not "return," for they are always here. The Hebrew god does not "return" (at least not until Christianity revises him) for he is everywhere. And of course animist societies have no need for "returning" gods because their gods are always here, in the souls of every object. Therefore, to claim "all" ancient cultures predict the return of the gods is only possible if you first disqualify every culture that doesn't believe it.

Ancient Texts!

Next up: *ancient texts!* There isn't really a lot of trust we can put in the *Popol Vuh* as an unbiased record of the Maya's beliefs, since it was only written down in 1588, long after Catholic influence infiltrated Mexico. Similarities to Genesis may well be the result of such contamination. Most scholars believe the opening lines, for example, are a Mayan translation of Genesis 1:1. It would be roughly the equivalent of trusting Shakespeare's *Julius Caesar* (written 1599) as an accurate representation of Roman history and beliefs. There is a foundation of truth, encrusted with later ideas. If we had no Roman history, we might never know which parts were true and which were Elizabethan fancies. I will wait for the *Ancient Aliens* episode on how Shakespeare encoded extraterrestrial knowledge into his plays—unless they were really written by *aliens!*

Snakes on a Spaceship!

Ancient Aliens doesn't have time for that now. Instead, we move on to *snakes!* What to make of the show's interest in flying serpents I can't say. Kukulkan isn't the Chinese dragon, as they suggest, since the Chinese dragon is *not* a serpent but a combination of nine animals: stag, camel, demon, snake, clam, carp, eagle, tiger, and cow. "Space clams" just doesn't feel the same. The serpent as a wisdom-bringer is nearly a human universal, probably because the shedding of its skin associated it with eternal youth and immortality. The only suggestion that Tsoukalos can make as to why this is relevant is that ancient people mistook spaceships for flying snakes and the emergence of astronauts from them as the "creation" of mankind.

Whatever. Tsoukalos claims that all world cultures have "not just similar but identical" serpent myths. "This is not coincidence. This is evidence for ancient alien encounters in the remote past. There is no other way." But this is so false as to be laughable. The serpent who steals immorality from Gilgamesh and/or Adam and Eve is not the Python slain by Apollo. The flying serpent god of Mexico is not the nine-part Chinese dragon. These creatures have vastly different stories and functions, and they have nothing to do with spaceships or delivering visitors from space. The Greeks, for example, had a serpent god of sorts, Zeus Meilichios, but he was a *subterranean* god, not a sky god. The Rainbow Serpent of the Australian aborigines lives in water, not the sky. Etc.

Boetian worshipper offering to a snake god. Note: Snake is emerging from a cave because spaceships come from underground. Wait, that's not right... (Photo: Jane Harrison, *Prolegomena to the Study of Greek Religion*, 1922)

The Fault, Dear Brutus, Is Not in Our Stars...

We finish up with a tour of Mayan astronomy, with von Däniken and Coppens arguing that the Maya's astronomical calculations are so sophisticated that (despite earlier praising their advanced math) they could not have "observed" or calculated these changes but must have been given them by the aliens—aliens who, incidentally, also neglected to inform them about such niceties as the heliocentric solar system, the outer planets, or the Big Bang. Heck, you'd think the aliens might have mentioned something about their home planet, or at least which star it orbited.

Of course, no Mayan conspiracy would be complete without the 2012 apocalypse claim, debunked so many times that it isn't funny. Childress says 2012 "might be the return of the gods themselves—the extraterrestrials." Obviously, Childress is *very* sincere when he insists he is *not* an ancient astronaut theorist. *Ancient Aliens* argued that the Maya "conspired" with the aliens to fix the date of the apocalypse and the destruction of the world. Nice of them to do so on behalf of the world. Apparently such contemporary figures as Charlemagne, Pope Leo III, Chinese emperor De Zong, and other luminaries weren't involved, since they betray no knowledge of the aliens. I wonder why the aliens chose only to appear to the Maya, or why this relatively isolated people were given the awesome task of fixing the end of the world on behalf of all humans. Heck, even the Tiwanaku weren't given a say, and they're the ones whose temple at Puma Punku is supposed to be an alien spaceport.

At any rate, with the deadline for the aliens' return or the end of the world or whatever just months after this episode's first airing, the episode did not seem designed to play well in reruns. Perhaps that's why the 2012 discussion was jammed at the end, near the closing credits, so it could be lopped off come 2013 and the series could replay the episode without later audiences being any the wiser that AATs once argued that the aliens would return in 2012. That kind of prediction worked so well when documentary filmmaker and AAT Alan Landsburg predicted their return for 2011.

EPISODE 2:
THE DOOMSDAY PROPHESIES
February 17, 2012

EPISODE REVIEW

Ancient Aliens had a two-hour, two-episode season premiere for Season Four, and suffice it to say, I was not willing to subject myself to that much *Ancient Aliens* in one sitting. I took a twenty-four hour break before watching "The Doomsday Prophesies," which aired exclusively on H2 following the simulcast of the premiere episode on History an hour earlier. This was the episode in which the program began promoting apparently fake PhDs as "experts."

I have less to say about this episode since it repeats much of the same pointless speculation about the Maya from the preceding hour, often in very similar arguments and wording. I think some footage may even be repeated. Fortunately, this time, the episode does try to place the Maya in historical context, noting that they flourished in the first millennium CE, contemporary with the Middle Ages in Europe—which is not exactly "rolling around in the mud," as one alternative theorist claimed. Surprisingly, the first H2 episode seems rather slower in pace, lingering on topics and driving the arguments into the ground through sheer repetition. How many times can one argue that the gods "came out of the sky" in one hour?

Sean-David Morton, "Ph.D.," of whom I've never heard, claimed that the Maya knew the center of the universe was a black hole one light year across. They did not. They knew there was a spot in the Milky Way that had no stars, and they considered it a hole in the sky, like many ancient people. Not the same as a black hole.

It appears that Mr. Morton is a psychic visionary who sells spiritual counseling, worked for psychic hotlines, and received a "Ph.D." from a school that appears in no directories and does not seem to exist. He claims on his website that his degree is from the "International Institute of Health and Spiritual Sciences in Montreal, Canada," but this school does not appear to be real. I suppose he means the "International Institute of Integral Human Sciences," which *is* in Montreal, but it does not grant degrees. Montreal has seven institutions licensed to grant degrees, and Morton's is not one of them. Morton most likely attended the International College of Spiritual and Psychic Sciences at the International Institute of Integral and Human Sciences, Montreal, which offers "various certificates equivalent to the bachelors, masters, or doctorate degrees." These are not accredited by Canada and are purely honorary. He apparently earned Certification Level V, described as "doctoral equivalent," in their "therapeutic counselling" program. The Certificate entitles the bearer to apply for an equivalency Ph.D. degree through a Sri Lankan university of complementary medicine (Open International University of Complimentary Medicines) whose degrees are not academically recognized outside Sri Lanka.

Morton also claims to attend the Astrological Sciences Institute at Exeter College, Oxford University, but according to the University, this does not exist either. Apparently, Morton is referring to the "Faculty of Astrological Studies," an independent group of astrologers with their own unaccredited degree program and who meet on the campus of Exeter College in the summer but are not affiliated with the College. Morton was accused in 2010 of bilking millions out of his followers by falsely claiming he could predict the stock market, and he sued UFOWatchDog.com for investigating him.

I publicly wrote after this episode aired that I was happy to correct the record when and if Mr. Morton could provide documentation of the Institute's existence and that his degree was awarded by a program accredited by a federally-recognized Canadian degree-granting institution. Instead, I received abusive communications from supporters of Mr. Morton, including one coming from what was claimed to be Mr. Morton's email address, making threats against me. (Note: Morton also claims to also have a doctorate in theology, but this is a D.Th. degree, not a Ph.D., so *Ancient Aliens* must be referring to his "therapeutic psychology" degree.)

So this is what happens when *Ancient Aliens* moves to H2: standards are now so low that accused psychic frauds now count as "experts," disingenuously described as "theologians" instead of "psychics."

Screen shot of *Ancient Aliens'* "The Doomsday Prophecies" documenting the show's endorsement of Sean-David Morton's "Ph.D." in an on-air chyron.

Much hay is made of the Mayan calendar, but again this is rather useless speculation about an imaginary end of the world. It is roughly as exciting as discovering when the Gregorian calendar turned from the second millennium to the third. The beginning of the calendar is attributed to Mayan knowledge of an asteroid that hit Austria in 3114 BCE—a rather specific and ridiculous claim. (Scholars suggest that a cuneiform tablet from 700 BCE documents an asteroid strike in Austria, known as the Köfels Impact Event, that according to computer models occurred around June 29, 3123 BCE; but: note the difference in day, month, and year.)

Morton and other ancient astronaut theorists (AATs) see the imaginary Mayan doomsday prophesies as confirmed by the Hopi prophecies, apparently ignorant of the fact that the Hopi were part of the same widespread cultural diffusion as the Maya and were influenced by Mesoamerican beliefs—including the Mexican view of the cycle of the ages.

Then we briefly discuss the end of days in Christian and Hindu myths, but there is no real effort to make a connection to aliens. But the show is confused about what it's trying to do. There is no real effort to distinguish between claims that 2012 is a Mayan doomsday or claims that 2012 is the year the aliens return. It certainly isn't the "end" of the calendar, as *Ancient Aliens* claims, since the Mayan Hanab-Pakal wrote of dates well beyond 2012.

Following this, we go back to the well about gods descending from the stars, just like in Episode 1, including the same blather about Kukulkan (Quetzalcoatl), the feathered serpent. Philip Coppens concludes that the feathered serpent must be a spaceship since humans can't emerge from serpents as the art seems to depict. Right. Talk about a false dichotomy. It's either an impossible record of a vomiting snake or a spaceship, nothing else. Even Robert Temple wasn't that stupid when he claimed Oannes, the Babylonian god who wore a fish-suit, was an amphibian from Sirius, not a man riding in a fish-shaped spaceship.

Giorgio Tsoukalos became very exciting about the Castillo temple at Chichen Itza, which annually creates the illusion of a serpent sliding down the stairs. This is a fine bit of art but hardly conclusive proof that the Maya (actually a post-Classic composite civilization from after 900 CE) were symbolizing alien space flights. This is doubly true when we realize that far from being the complex and elaborate temple the AATs imagine was built all at once to honor the god, in fact El Castillo as we know it today was built atop several earlier and smaller pyramids, encasing each in successive layers. This one happens to be particularly impressive because its size made it possible to include 365 steps and the serpent illusion. The temple was completed perhaps as late as the twelfth century CE, around the same time as Europe's great cathedrals. This is not a particularly ancient site, so we are left with another impossible choice: Did the Maya simply remember for three or four thousand years exactly what happened when the aliens arrived, or did the aliens pop in and out of Mexico between 600 and 1200 CE while skipping the Christian and Islamic lands? Aliens are not much for monotheists.

El Castillo as photographed by Teobert Maler in 1892. (Wikimedia Commons)

Tsoukalos also claims the Mayan god Bolon Yokte K'Uh ("God of Nine Strides") is described in the "ancient texts" as "shiny" and "glowing"—an actual description of an ancient alien. This would be great if there were any indication this was so, but as the archaeologist immediately preceding him notes, we know almost nothing about this god. A rare Classic Maya text to mention him is heavily damaged, and I can find no evidence that he is described as glowing or shiny. The closest I can come is the occasional association of Bolon Yokte with the moon (whose glyph is also the signal for the possessive case, like an apostrophe in English) in some older, less accurate scholarly texts. Some think Bolon Yokte might actually be multiple gods, the Nine Lords of the Night.

Now, here's the rub: The inscription mentioning Bolon Yokte referenced above is the same one that lists the date of 2012 with its world-changing events. A new translation makes clear that the event of 2012 is not the end of the world, but a parade in which the statue of Bolon Yokte will receive a new robe.

The other texts discussed, the so-called Books of Chilam Balam, were something I had never heard of. It turns out there is a good reason for that. These books (and there are several) were written in the late seventeenth and early eighteenth centuries. While they contain some stories that date back to the conquest period or before, they are also very much documents of eighteenth century Mayan life and belief—not records of spacemen from 3114 BCE. They describe, for example, the coming of the Europeans. Here, Bolon Yokte isn't exactly an astronaut. As Ralph Roys translates: "The drum and rattle of Ah Bolon-yocte shall resound. At that time there shall be the green [i.e., first] turkey. [...] They shall find their food among the trees." Aliens invented Thanksgiving.

But no matter. According to the AATs of *Ancient Aliens*, the end of the Mayan long count calendar in December 2012 would offer only two choices: the end of the world or the return of the aliens. Childress, summing up, makes this nonsensical claim: "It's hard to know the future—what's going to happen at the end of 2012—but it seems that perhaps the Mayans had some glimpse into the future that we have yet to find out." Remember that, and hold the AATs (especially David Childress) accountable for nothing happening on that long-marked day.

Heaven help us, Giorgio Tsoukalos was actually the voice of reason, chiding doomsday theorists and correctly (!) stating that the Mayan calendar round simply begins anew in 2012, with no consequences whatsoever for the earth.

So why did we have to sit through this hour of admitted nonsense?

EPISODE 3:
THE GREYS
February 24, 2012

EPISODE REVIEW

Just before this episode aired, ancient astronaut theorist (AAT) Giorgio Tsoukalos tweeted that *Ancient Aliens*' ratings were as high as ever after the move to H2. This was not entirely true. One of the two episodes that aired on premier night was simulcast on H2 and the original flavor History Channel. That episode scored 1.4 million viewers and ranked eleventh for the night among total viewers across all cable broadcasts, on par with last season. The subsequent H2-only episode did not rank in the top 22 according to published rankings of the top 20 cable shows (two ties made for 22 shows). That means, logically, that the episode's ratings had to be lower than the 22nd-ranked show, which had only 52,000 viewers. Either that or Nielsen does not report H2's ratings. Either way, Tsoukalos's statement is either dissembling (leaving out H2) or ignorant (not knowing H2's ratings).

The move to H2 certainly did nothing to improve the quality of *Ancient Aliens*. In the opening moments of "The Greys," David Childress falsely claims that elongated skulls (produced by the well-known ritual of head binding) are in fact "half alien, half-human" hybrids. This is stupid beyond words. But more on that later!

First we start with the Roswell "UFO" crash, which has been debunked so many times that even many ufologists don't believe it was an alien spacecraft anymore. This doesn't stop *Ancient Aliens* from asserting flatly that "alien bodies" were retrieved from a UFO in 1947, all of which is a complete and utter fabrication. Then we move on to the equally debunked Betty and Barney Hill abduction, retelling the Hills' story at face value, with none of the troubling problems with their story ever mentioned. Following this, we have more warmed over recent alien abduction stories, including the alleged hybrid children, which, if I understand the blonde abductee correctly, involves two eggs and two sperm to make one hybrid child. What any of this has to do with "ancient" aliens I have no idea. This belongs to modern ufology and conspiracy theorizing rather than the ancient astronaut theory.

The takeaway is that the theorists on the show believe that if enough people say the Grey aliens are real, they must be.

Finally we reach the connection to ancient astronauts: Giorgio Tsoukalos says some statues and cave drawings look like "Grey" aliens because they have large, black eyes. This would, of course, make many cats Grey aliens, too. Needless to say, this is another case of seeing what one wants to see in ambiguous images that could be read many ways. Many of the images the show presents as "Greys," incidentally, have white eyes rather than black, or eyes that were square or otherwise atypical for "Greys." Besides, didn't we learn last week that aliens wore helmets and needed breathing apparatuses to survive?

Grey alien. © 2005 Jason Colavito.

Jason Martell claims that the Anunnaki are partners with the Grey aliens, but his claims are only warmed over Zecharia Sitchin. The actual Sumerian and Babylonian texts say nothing like what the theorists claims. The Anunnaki are referenced only occasionally, and then in contradictory ways. As I noted before, the Anunnaki are best attested as gods created by Marduk and who live underground. Only in Sitchin do they become spacefaring conquistadors. But this does give us a doozy of a quote from David Childress: "When you look at the evidence, it appears there were a number of different aliens species that were coming to this planet." *Now* will he finally admit he's an ancient astronaut theorist?

> "Nearly all of the 'ancient astronaut' evidence that can be found in the hundreds of books on the subject, can be alternatively explained in the time travel hypothesis, and have been."
>
> DAVID CHILDRESS, *The Time-Travel Handbook* (1999)

Hopi *paatuwvota*, or "magic flying shields," are then likened to UFOs because they are round and transport shamans into the sky. But they left out the part that in Hopi culture these *paatuwvota* are small and woven from cotton in the manner of wedding dress. The Hopi also believe that certain types of gourds can fly when a supernatural being straddles them. Anthropologists believe these flying cloths and gourds represent the shaman's trance state, where, in communion with the spirit world, the shaman feels he is able to fly. This is the same neurological reaction that can make people high on some drugs (ketamine, PCP, etc.) feel that they are flying. So unless aliens also are into PCP, it's probably not a UFO.

Now we're back to the elongated skulls, which Childress claims are alien hybrids because "recent DNA tests" prove they are "half human and half some other race." I can't find any evidence of these DNA tests. The best I can find is that one test on a mummy produced inconclusive results because there was not enough viable DNA to complete the test. Either that or Childress believed a November 2011 *Daily Mail* story that DNA tests were going to be conducted on an "alien" mummy from Peru. And what would non-human DNA look like? How would it mesh with the 23 human chromosomes the "hybrid" would have? In fact, these elongated skulls are produced by intentional (human) cranial deformation, which we know because it is still practiced today in places like Vanuatu, and was practiced and described in historic times.

Painting by Paul Kane showing Flathead Indian deforming a child's skull through head-binding. Clearly, having sex with aliens would be faster.

Just for kicks, here is Hippocrates proving Childress wrong back in ancient Greek times (though, note, Hippocrates was apparently a Lamarckian):

> And first of the *Macrocephali* or *Long-heads;* a Nation whose Heads are different from all the world. At first the length of their Heads was owing to a *Law* or *Custom,* but now *Nature* herself conforms to the *Custom;* it being an opinion among 'em, that those who have the longest Heads

are the most noble. The *Custom* stood thus. As soon as the Child was born, they immediately fashion'd the soft and tender Head of it with their Hands, and, by the use of *bandages and proper arts,* forc'd it to grow lengthwise; by which means the sphærical figure of the Head was perverted, and the length increas'd.

("Of Air, Water, and Situation", trans. Francis Clifton)

Up next we pretend along with Erich von Däniken that Mars had a civilization 10,000 years ago and came to earth to do battle. Philip Coppens then claims our (alien) "DNA" drives us to go to Mars, which he says has always been seen as earth's twin—impossible since most cultures did not recognize Mars as a planet in our sense but rather merely as a red light in the sky (remember: they thought the sun was a flaming chariot). Mars is associated with war not because evil aliens conquered earth from there but because it is red, the color of blood. But even that is not well-established. The Roman Mars was originally an agricultural and fertility god. In Mesopotamia, the planet Mars was associated with Nergal, a war god yes, but one associated with the setting sun—hence his association with the color red and Mars. But far from "earth's twin," in Babylon Mars was considered the planet of ill-omen and bad luck (its Babylonian name means "death omen"), so it's doubtful these people—heirs of the Anunnaki remember—wanted to go there.

We speculate next on life on other planets (sure, why not) before moving on to Teotihuacan, which Giorgio Tsoukalos fails to notice is the much later Aztec name, not the original one, of the site they called "the place where the gods meet," so the name carries little weight as the meeting place of the aliens. Von Däniken repeats an old canard that Teotihuacan is a perfect scale model of the solar system, but it isn't. Such claims work only by cherry pick-

> "Around the principal pyramids are a great number of smaller ones, rarely exceeding thirty feet in height, which, according to tradition, were dedicated to the stars, and served as sepulchres for the great men of the nation. They are arranged symmetrically in avenues terminating at the sides of the great pyramids, which face the cardinal points. The plain on which they stand was called Micoatl, or 'Path of the Dead.'"
>
> WILLIAM HICKLING PRESCOTT, *History of the Conquest of Mexico* (1850)

ing buildings large and small, while leaving out many others. They took just nine of more than seventy temple platforms to make their correlation. Similarly, the fake claim that ancient pyramids form of a perfect world grid pattern across the planet is also a fraud, one made by cherry picking sites to fit a predetermined idea. But we've been over the grid thing before on *Ancient Aliens*.

Oh, yeah... we were supposed to be talking about Grey aliens, weren't we? Well forget about that! Now we need to talk about the "Reptilians," David Icke's silly idea that lizard people have been running the world for a few thousand years. According to *Ancient Aliens*, the "Reptilians" are actually Grey aliens in disguise. Here we repeat all the same lies about Quetzalcoatl and other snake gods from the last two episodes. There is no need to review them again.

The added wrinkle is that this time, the Greys were reproducing with dinosaurs or reptiles to make "Reptilians." This is Theosophy's old root race lies recast in technological clothes. This whole story is simply taken from Blavatsky's fraud. George Noory adds that Satan was a "reptilian extraterrestrial," but you know, whatever. He has

> **THEOSOPHY ON REPTILIAN ANCESTORS**
>
> *"Now why has less change taken place in Australia than elsewhere? Where is the raison d'être for such a 'curse of retardation'? It is simply because the nature of the environment develops pari passu with the race concerned. Correspondences rule in every quarter. The survivors of those later Lemurians, who escaped the destruction of their fellows when the main continent was submerged, became the ancestors of a portion of the present native tribes. Being a very low sub-race, begotten originally of animals, of monsters, whose very fossils are now resting miles under the sea floors, their stock has since existed in an environment strongly subjected to the law of retardation."*
>
> HELENA BLAVATSKY, *The Secret Doctrine* (1888)

serpentine traits because he was, you know, *the serpent* from the Garden of Eden in Christian myth. Serpent worship emerges from, you know, *serpents*, not from aliens. The serpent was worshiped because the shedding of its skin made it seem as though snakes had the secret of immortality.

The programs kept promising specific myths that documented encounters with supernatural hybrid creatures "produced by Grey aliens," but they couldn't really find one. Dragons are not lizard people. (In fact, the talking heads seem ignorant of the fact that the modern dragon is not terribly old. Prior to the Middle Ages, the "dragon" in Western thought was merely a giant snake. As mentioned before, the Chinese dragon is *not a reptile*.)

I fail to understand how an alien that the theorists claim is about three feet tall somehow has a head with a "brain capacity" far beyond our own, since even by the most generous estimates, at the size listed for the aliens, their heads couldn't be much bigger than ours.

In the end, the talking heads can't decide whether Grey "space brother" aliens actually had sex with humans, genetically engineered us and several other species, or "altered" ape DNA to make humans as alien hybrids ourselves. The concluding speculation about evolution, aliens, and the future direction of the human race is rather pointless since there is no evidence for the existence of the aliens in the first place. But either way, futurism has nothing to do with ancient history unless the final silly claim is true: the aliens are *time travelers* from *our own future*! In which case, human history is one big incestuous loop from which apparently our DNA emerged *ex nihilo* as a result of a time travel paradox.

The biggest paradox is how one show can have so many discordant ideas and imagine it is telling a single coherent story.

EPISODE 4:
ALIENS AND MEGA-DISASTERS
MARCH 2, 2012

EPISODE REVIEW

A*NCIENT ALIENS* HAS NEVER BEEN SUBTLE, but airing in a week when tornadoes killed dozens across the United States, having a bunch of ignorant know-nothings argue that aliens cause natural disasters, including the devastating Japanese earthquake and tsunami of 2011 and the Haitian earthquake of 2010, is just disgusting.

"Aliens and Mega-Disasters" argues that aliens "may" have had a hand in volcanic eruptions, earthquakes, tsunamis, and other natural cataclysms, including the asteroid strike that killed off the dinosaurs "on purpose." How the aliens would know that the mammals which 65 million years later would give rise to humans would not also die, I can only imagine. Why the aliens waited 65 million years to create humans, I also could not possibly fathom.

Now, here I have to confess that geology is not my area, so I have a bit less to say this time around. Of course, geology isn't the ancient astronaut theorists' area either. No type of science is their area. As we shall see, by the end of this episode these theorists have once again *misinterpreted and fabricated facts* to create false "proof" that the aliens warned the Chinese about a meteoric impact in 3116 BCE. But more on that anon…

We begin across the East China Sea in Japan. According to David ("I'm not an ancient astronaut theorist") Childress, sightings of strange sky lights in Japan on tsunami day ("UFOs") prove that aliens are behind it all:

> You have to think, are the extraterrestrials particularly interested in what happens to us in certain catastrophes and life-changing events

that are occurring on this planet. And it's possible that the extraterrestrials themselves are influencing some of these events.

Of course, the fact that "earthquake lights" are a well-known result of the geological forces that create earthquakes is briefly discussed only to be rejected by "ancient astronaut theorists" because they do not understand geology. Obviously UFOs are a more logical explanation.

Now, here is where the "ancient" aliens come in. Earthquakes, you see, also happened in ancient times, and ancient Greeks believed Poseidon caused earthquakes; since gods are aliens, aliens cause earthquakes. Q.E.D. According to Childress, Poseidon, the alien, was apparently upset about the Christianization of Crete so he destroyed all the pagans in Crete with an earthquake and tsunami in 365 CE, letting Christians take over the world. No, this does not make sense, but David Childress rarely makes any sense.

According to Childress, Poseidon's trident is an alien weapon: "You have to wonder if this trident wasn't some kind of high-tech, extraterrestrial device." No, I don't. In fact, the earliest images of Poseidon depict him holding a lotus-bud, which was later stylized into a trident. So, unless you believe in flower power, this isn't particularly compelling alien evidence.

Forbidden Archaeology author Michael Cremo, the Hindu creationist (and now apparently ancient astronaut theorist), then finds it fascinating that the US Navy named elements of the nuclear submarine program after Poseidon and his trident, thus "proving" that the U.S. government is in a conspiracy with aliens who pretended to be Greek gods. This leads to an irrelevant discussion of whether the U.S. government is "weaponizing" weather; there is nothing alien about this, so I will skip it.

> The city of Shurippak, a city which, as thou knowest,
> Is situated on the bank of the river Euphrates.
> That city was corrupt, so that the gods within it
> Decided to bring about a deluge
>
> EPIC OF GILGAMESH, trans. William Muss-Arnolt

The ancient flood myths of Mesopotamia and the Bible are then discussed, though the *Epic of Gilgamesh* is wrongly attributed to Sumer (it's Akkadian/Babylonian, compiled from originally unrelated Sumerian poems). What's the point of bothering to critique theories that aliens weaponized the weather to create the ancient Flood since there is not a shred of geological evidence that this flood ever happened? *Pace,* Graham Hancock, whose ghostly visage rises up to claim relevance in an age where ancient astronauts have superseded his 1990s-era lost civilization theory. Giorgio Tsoukalos pops up to claim there were two groups of aliens, good and bad, who alternately protected some humans and destroyed the rest (as per *Gilgamesh*), but, you know, whatever: no flood, no reason to invent an explanation for a flood.

Then suddenly we move on to claims that a volcano in Indonesia inspired Buddhist stupas, which Tsoukalos and Philip Coppens claim (well, ask leading questions that sound like claims) are depictions of UFOs. Volcano gods, you see, are actually aliens who live in volcanoes. (Isn't that Scientology?) Tsoukalos claims extraterrestrials "descended from the sky in

> "[T]he ... volcanoes, the explosions, the Galactic confederation 75 million years ago, and a gentleman by the name Xemu there. Those are not trade secrets."
>
> WARREN MCSHANE, Scientologist, court transcripts (1995)

nuts and bolts spaceships" to go into volcanoes. I'm not sure how even an alien spaceship could withstand the heat inside active volcanoes. According to Childress, they are "bases" for extraterrestrials, who would erupt the volcano to keep people away from their volcano villain lairs.

Tsoukalos notes that ancient people worshiped nature, which even he realizes makes it sound like the aliens aren't necessary to explain volcano gods. This is why he then adds: "However, there was a fine line between worshiping nature and worshiping something else—and that something else was extraterrestrials." But why? If you concede nature worship, the alien explanation becomes redundant and unnecessary.

Childress is shocked that climate change has led to desertification of the Sahara. Cave art there depicts shamans wearing animal masks, which Childress and Tsoukalos insist on seeing as astronauts wearing space suits. "The look exactly like extraterrestrials," said Childress. Oh, really? Have you seen any to compare? Please share.

Childress then goes back to the debunked well of the Dogon to discuss Robert Temple's fraudulent 1976 *Sirius Mystery*. The tribal legends cited are problematic at best (the Sirius lore does not exist; it was the invention of deluded French anthropologists), and *contra Ancient Aliens*, the "spaceship" the Dogon's gods used to descend from space was not a UFO. Dogon legends clearly describe it as an ark, and it is well-known that Christian and Islamic contamination from the Noah's ark story contributed to this legend. So, in short, this whole segment on the Dogon contains lies and distortions debunked more than 20 years earlier (by Walter van Beek, in 1991), as I reported in *The Cult of Alien Gods* (2005), and they just keep on rolling with it as though newer research never happened.

Guess what: The almost certainly fake Ph.D. Sean-David Morton, whom we met in Episode 2, is back again, now claiming that wooly mammoths were "flash-frozen" by a comet, a debunked claim from Immanuel Velikovsky. Tsoukalos then claims that by assuming an ancient Hongshan carving of a comet at Chifeng was created before the comet struck (116 years before, to be exact), we can "prove" that the aliens warned the ancients about it. If I assume ancient astronaut theorists are actually ferns, I can then "prove" that they perform photosynthesis. (The "comet" in question, "Proto-Encke," is typically believed to have had remnants of its tail strike around 3150 BCE; the artificially exact 3113-3116 date has been arbitrarily created by alternative theorists to harmonize with the start of the Mayan calendar in 3114 BCE. (Yes, I know it was an Austrian meteor the Maya supposedly marked in an earlier episode, but consistency is not *Ancient Aliens*' strong suit.) Other estimates put collisions with its tail in 2000 BCE or any number of other dates. Encke orbits the sun every three years.)

But I can't really see what the reason is for suggesting that the carving is older than the comet collision it supposedly depicts. I watched the segment several times, and I can't make heads or tails of it. Here are the facts the show presents:

- The Hongshan carvings are around 5000 years old. (Discovered in 2011, this would date them to 2989 BCE in absolute terms, but *Ancient Aliens* miscalculates this as 3000 BCE.)

- The comet struck between "3113 and 3116 BCE" according to Morton of the dubious Ph.D. (though, as we have seen, the better date estimate is closer to 3150 BCE).

- The narrator then states that the carving depicts a comet that would not strike "for another 116 years."

How does that even make sense? 3116 BCE happened *before* 3000 BCE, not after. The carving would be 116 years *younger* than the fireball since BCE dates count down, not up. Worse, the more accurate dates of 3150 BCE and 2989 BCE respectively only compound the error. And either way, the Hongshan carving's date is *approximate*, not absolute. I checked the Chinese archaeological reports from August of 2011 when the carving was discovered, along with Xinhua news coverage of them, and they confirm that the date is an *estimate*, not an absolute. So this is another case of ancient astronaut theorists combining arrogance and ignorance to create fake evidence.

The final few minutes break down into a series of frenzied, weird claims that the aliens want to punish us for our...wait for it... "arrogance and ignorance," in the words of Erich von Däniken. Fat chance! *Ancient Aliens* is still on, isn't it?

EPISODE 5:
THE NASA CONNECTION
March 9, 2012

EPISODE REVIEW

THIS EPISODE CONTINUED the trend of *Ancient Aliens* moving ever farther away from its core concept, largely because there is so little to the ancient astronaut theory that it quickly becomes repetitive. This episode focuses on whether NASA is engaged in a conspiracy to suppress evidence of UFOs, ancient astronauts, and alien monuments on the moon and Mars.

I'll be frank: ufology is not my particular area of expertise, and I don't particularly care much about evidence-free claims that since astronauts saw shiny lights in space these had to be alien spacecraft. Since there is almost nothing "ancient" in tonight's *Ancient Aliens*, I'll leave it to ufology skeptics to offer more substantive critiques of the program's twisting of recent history. I will devote most of my comments to the occasional claims about ancient history.

The Moon

Several astronauts, including Buzz Aldrin, Edgar Mitchell, and Story Musgrave, show up to talk about the moon landing, and we get a potted history of NASA's moon missions, with the added coda from David Childress that the astronauts of Apollo 11 were tasked with secretly photographing "certain parts of the moon" with "artificial structures," for which no evidence is given. I presume this refers to Childress' silly book about the topic, *Extraterrestrial Archaeology* (2000), which Childress claimed in 2006 was *not* about alien archaeology even though it was about archaeological sites on the moon and Mars. Mitchell is well-known for his belief in UFOs.

Much hay is made of the fact that the father of the man who chose Apollo 11's landing spot was an Egyptologist specializing in

Egyptian religion. Apparently, conspiracy theorists feel this means that NASA chose a landing spot to align with Orion's belt to honor the god Osiris. Even if this was true, so what? The tallest mountain on Mars is named for the Greek Olympus, but this doesn't make it a conspiracy to promote Zeus worship. Nor, for that matter, does the fact that the very planets themselves bear the names of Roman gods. After all, didn't *Ancient Aliens* tell us last year that the Greco-Roman gods were laser-wielding space aliens who landed a UFO on the (Greek) Olympus?

Then we hear from Michael Bara that Buzz Aldrin and Neil Armstrong performed a Freemason offering to Osiris of poured wine and broken bread. Really? How did that work? Everything that went up on Apollo 11 was carefully weighed and measured, and wine wasn't on that list. Bara proposes that Catholic communion is a rite of Osiris, a rather simplistic reduction of a widespread rite of libation. I don't really know anything about Michael Bara except that he shows up across the internet as a proponent of the Face on Mars and to imagine conspiracies of scientists and historians who suppress alien influence to further their careers, as he wrote on the EnterpriseMission.com website:

> The Internet is a major threat to the Guilded [sic] cloister of the "peer reviewed journals" by providing an outlet for ideas rejected - not on their merits - but perhaps because of the jeopardy in which they place established careers and well funded laboratories.

Because scientists are getting so rich off faking carbon dates on wood chips.

NASA's own incompetence, losing the original recordings of Apollo 11, is seen as part of a conspiracy, even though an intentionally degraded version of those recordings was broadcasted live on television in 1969 with nary an alien in sight. (The degraded signal was necessary to meet television's technical capacity at the time.) But at least it wasn't a "moon landing hoax" conspiracy.

Mars

Erich von Däniken starts talking about the Face on Mars, long debunked, and supposed "pyramids" on Mars. But he says that he doesn't know what to think is true because it's all so mysterious. These "structures," really geological formations, would, if artificial, have to be the largest buildings known in the universe to be big enough to see from space. Strangely, this area of "research" is quickly glossed over, probably due to a lack of public domain video of Mars compared to the hours of moon landing tapes. At any rate, this section was redolent of Graham Hancock and Robert Bauval's 1998 anti-NASA tract, *The Mars Mystery*.

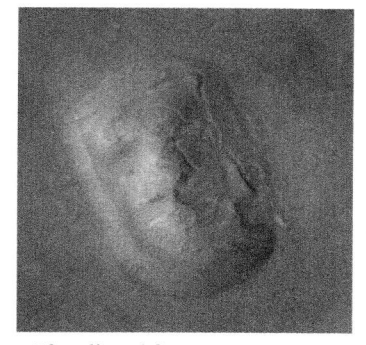

The alleged face on Mars as photographed by Mars Global Surveyor in 2001. (NASA/JPL)

Space Shuttle UFOs

NASA has a "direct pipeline" to the aliens, according to the show, which then offered discussions of flashing lights and other space anomalies witnessed from the space shuttle. These videos have become famous in UFO circles, but skeptics have discussed and explained them. At any rate, modern UFOs aren't my field, and I don't have much to add their discussions. When Childress describes "extraterrestrials in special suits" looking like luminous angels with wings ("in space!" he adds) viewed from a Russian voyage, the only thing I could think of was Lovecraft's Elder Things from *At the Mountains of Madness* sailing across space on their wings: "They seemed able to traverse the interstellar ether on their vast membranous wings—thus oddly confirming some curious hill folklore long ago told me by an antiquarian colleague."

Conspiracy

Michael Bara claims that NASA is engaged in a government-mandated program of controlling information and suppressing evidence of extraterrestrial contact. This is all well-trod territory for ufology buffs, and then Bara claims that NASA is run by secret societies whose members believe themselves to be physical descendents of the Egyptian gods, who are space aliens. This connects, he says, to Freemasonry and the Hermetic Order of the Golden Dawn. These groups, supposedly, descend from the Illuminati and a succession of secret societies stretching back to Egypt.

But these societies have nothing to do with space aliens. The Golden Dawn was Aleister Crowley's (first) group, and his thing was ritual magic, not extraterrestrials. It's only in Lovecraftian chaos magick that Crowley's magical beings are married to space aliens, though, interestingly, Lovecraft's beings were influenced by the Celtic creatures used by Arthur Machen, another member of the Golden Dawn. But he didn't have aliens either.

Somehow, the Apollo space mission's very logo is roped into the conspiracy, with the "A" representing not Apollo but Asar (a variant spelling of Usir, or Osiris). The symbol of the Mercury missions is falsely said to be an Egyptian ankh; it is in fact the astronomical symbol for Mercury, used since the Middle Ages and combining the symbol for Venus with horns representing the god Mercury's winged cap. But even if they were Egyptian, so what? Using Egyptian motifs does not equal space aliens. If that were true, then the Chrysler Building, whose lobby is decorated in Egyptian-influenced Deco style, would be the world's tallest monument to space aliens. But this is passed over quickly so we can get to *Nazis!* The show discusses Werner von Braun, a former Nazi turned NASA rocket scientist, because he was interested in space and had—and this is damning—read *War of the Worlds* and thus believed aliens could exist on Mars. A very long segment talks about his rocketry with nary a hint of why this is relevant to ancient aliens.

Von Braun was supposedly obsessed with the Norse god Týr (Germanic Ziu or Tiwaz), but *contra* the narration, Týr was not a sky god who "ruled over Mars" and provided "technology" to humans. Týr derives from the same proto-Indo-European root as Zeus and the Vedic Dyaus, *Dyeus*, who was originally the god of the daytime sky. Týr's onetime position at the head of the pantheon was usurped by Odin after the Migration Age. He did not "rule" Mars; he was equated with the *god* Mars in the *interpretatio romana* because both were gods of war, but this was an attempt to create Latin equivalents for the Norse gods; it did *not* mean that the Germans saw him as the god of the *planet* Mars. This correlation is why the Roman day of Mars became our Day of Týr, or Tuesday.

Nor did the Nazis believe that Aryans came from the stars and were aliens from space. Nazi ideology referred to the Aryan homeland of Thule, an earthly island and a kind of German Atlantis, one of superior ancient technology, deep connections to the cosmos, and superior scientific knowledge. ... Wait a minute: isn't that what *An-*

cient Aliens is all about? I see why they want to ignore this. *Did ancient aliens support Nazism?* American viewers demand answers.

The final segment talks about advanced propulsion systems that really have nothing to do with ancient aliens except that a bunch conspiracy theorists think that we are reverse engineering UFO technology to build anti-gravity craft. Once again David ("I'm not an ancient astronaut theorist!") Childress spent the entire segment talking about "retro-engineered spacecraft" from many different types of aliens. We conclude with irrelevant speculation about terraforming Mars and eliding the potential discovery of "life" on other planets (which could take any form, such as bacteria) with "a prior advanced civilization." Michael Bara concludes that NASA exists to prove that elite humans are the descendants of the main Egyptian gods.

Of course this is ridiculous. Everyone knows elite humans are descendants of lizard people from the Nameless City in the deserts of Saudi Arabia. You know it's true. David Icke was even on this episode of *Ancient Aliens. Coincidence?*

EPISODE 6:
THE MYSTERIES OF PUMA PUNKU
MARCH 16, 2012

EPISODE REVIEW

Well, this was different. This episode of *Ancient Aliens* focused on a single site, Puma Punku in Bolivia, rehashing the exact same material first presented in the 2009 pilot episode. That material was carefully debunked by the podcasters Dumbass and Skeptoid, and there is nothing in this episode that hasn't been refuted countless times since the first alternative interpretations of the site began in the early twentieth century.

I'm not sure why the show chooses to refer to the Tiwanaku site by the name of Puma Punku, which is actually the name of one of the monumental centers at the site (it's closer to the other temples at Tiwanaku than the Pentagon is to the Capitol), except that it makes it sound different from the 2009, 2010, and 2011 *Ancient Aliens* episodes analyzing Tiwanaku.

Chief alien enthusiast Giorgio Tsoukalos summed it up: "Puma Punku is the only site on planet earth that in my opinion was built directly by extraterrestrials."

Prove it.

Since 2009 you haven't provided a shred of proof of anything extraterrestrial at the site, and you didn't do it this time, either.

When the Stars Are Right

Before we get into the specific nuttiness of this episode of *Ancient Aliens*, let's begin with a disclaimer: Tiwanaku is not 17,000 years old. This date derives from the work of Arthur Posnansky, who tried to apply archaeoastronomy to the site but did so in ways that modern scholars do not recognize as legitimate. Posnansky proposed a date of 15,000 B.P. (before present, i.e. 13,000 BCE), which the geniuses at *Ancient Aliens* misread as 15,000 BCE (i.e., Before the Common Era, formerly known as BC, or Before Christ), adding an extra 2,000 years onto Posnansky's already flawed dates.

Here's what he did wrong. Posnansky *assumed* that the Kalasasaya temple at Tiwanaku was laid out with perfect accuracy to align to the equinoxes and solstices that he felt (but could not prove) were important to the Tiwanaku people. Thus, on a certain day the sun was supposed to rise above one rock at the temple and set behind another. (Ah, but which rock should we use?) Since the current ruins do not align with these celestial events accurately, he concluded that the ruins must have been built at a time when they *would have aligned* with that event. Since the sun and sky change positions at a predictable rate due to gradual changes in the angle of

The Gate of the Sun, Tiwanaku. (Library of Congress)

the earth's axis, he concluded that the Kalassaya was built in 13,000 BCE as a solar observatory, despite no other evidence of solar astronomy at the site.

The sheer number of assumptions was something of a tip off that his method was flawed, and no other method of dating confirms the dates. (Carbon dating of artifacts at the site places construction around 200 CE. There are no 14,000-year-old artifacts ever dated from Tiwanaku. Surely aliens would have left *something* from all their time living there.) Worse, the temple actually aligns perfectly with the spring and autumnal equinox *right now*, bisected by the sun's beams on those two days. There is therefore no reason to propose a 13,000 BCE construction date to solve a problem that does not exist.

The long and short of it is that Posnansky *assumed* celestial alignments and *assumed* flawless construction and then used his assumptions to "prove" that his assumptions were correct.

Now, funny thing: Posnansky dated the Kalasasaya, which is a different temple from the Puma Punka temple, though both are part of Tiwanaku. *Ancient Aliens* even gets its pseudoscience wrong.

So, if Puma Punku is not 15,000 years old, then the rest of the episode's speculation is rather fruitless unless one thinks that the aliens were flying around the early medieval world and *nobody noticed.* Oh, and 600 CE wasn't that long ago, so we ought to have traces of their landing sites, the trash they threw out, *something*. But, no. Not a trace.

H-Blocks: The History Channel of the Gods

Ok, so we move on to the show's actual silly claims. After an opening segment dedicated to making us accept Posnansky's flawed date, David Childress tries to prove that the granite blocks at the site are cut at "precision angles," but his demonstration fails when his set square fails to align precisely with the block, which is out of true by a few degrees.

Giorgio Tsoukalos then argues, as he did in 2009, that diamond-tipped drills made the stones, even though he concedes in a spectacularly silly field piece at Chris Dunn's workroom that the surface *looks nothing like diamond cut surfaces*, arguing instead that the original diamond-cut surfaces he *assumed* existed must have eroded later. Sigh.

Childress then argues that a line of H-shaped blocks at Puma Punku that resemble the History and H2 logos is "beyond what we can do today," but once again this is not true. The Aztecs, a historical people, managed to carve precise and pretty blocks with precision on their temples and no one claims aliens built the Templo Mayor. The Romans, at the same time as Tiwanaku, also managed to do without "levitation and antigravity" and "super-technology" that Childress attributes to the ancient aliens. In fact, the architectural techniques used at Puma Punku are common across Middle Horizon (600-900 CE) sites in the region. The site is not unique.

According to Tsoukalos and Erich von Däniken, Puma Punku is the aliens' very own building, while Tiwanaku is a human-built visitors' center for worshipping the aliens. Childress then states that the sculptured heads on the walls of the Kalasasaya represent all human races, including Grey aliens (even though they have noses). These are in actuality very stylized human sculptures and cannot be related to any anatomical humans, as professional sculptor and alternative theorist Brien Foerster seems to think. "All cultures on earth" did not accept Tiwanaku as special, as Philip Coppens claims, since no one outside South America had any idea of its existence.

Childress is also wrong that Native Americans cannot grow facial hair so therefore Tiwanaku statues with facial hair must be visitors from Europe or space. At right is a Native American with a mustache and beard.

Aliens Speak Sumerian

Childress also gets quite excited about the "Fuente Magna" bowl, a purported artifact from near Lake Titicaca in Bolivia that supposedly shows "proto-Sumerian" and Semitic writing alongside South American designs. (Childress is wrong about it having *both* Sumerian and proto-Sumerian; two linguists merely disagreed on whether it was Sumerian or proto-Sumerian.) It was found at an unknown date (sometime prior to 1958) and brought to the attention of archaeologists sometime between 1958 and 1960. No one paid attention to it until 2000, when a documentary crew for *Atlantis in the Andes* filmed it. Given the extremely problematic provenance, it is most likely a hoax, like the Kensington Rune Stone and other supposed "evidence" of Old World peoples in the Americas. Today, some Mormons celebrate the artifact as proof of the Book of Mormon. Interestingly, Mormons began working in nearby Peru in 1956, just at the time this "proof" was supposedly uncovered.

David Childress says Native Americans can't grow facial hair. General Ely S. Parker disagrees.

But no matter the truth, the bowl fails to support, as Childress claims, Zecharia Sitchin's theories of alien Anunnaki in Bolivia since the inscription, when "translated," refers to either (a) Sumerians teaching the Bolivians goat-herding, with no aliens in sight or (b) a purification rite, again with no aliens. It depends on which translator of the likely fake inscription you prefer. (One of the two translators, Afrocentrist writer Clyde Winters, insists that the Inca are identical with Enki, the Sumerian god, because, well, they sound alike. Quality work.) At best, the bowl would be evidence for trans-Atlantic contact. But it's probably a hoax.

"Super-Technology"

Tsoukalos argues for a "potential yes" to the use of sonic technology at Puma Punku because a legend current in 1550 (500 years after abandonment of the site) claimed giants used trumpets to move the stones. The Greeks thought the Mycenaean ruins were built by Cyclopes, and medieval people thought Merlin made Stonehenge fly from Ireland to England. Late legends are not reliable sources. This does not stop David Childress:

> It's part of our idea, too, that some giant airship that was a factory with power tools and power saws and routers and drills just landed here and began processing these giant blocks of stone and then ultimately created Puma Punku.

We then get into claims that the site was a factory for creating energy (?) which was built by electric drills because the stones are carved so precisely. Childress calls it "the kind of granite spaceport that extraterrestrials would want."

"Planning means writing," von Däniken said, arguing for why "primitive" (read: stupid) Aymara Indians could not have built the site. No, it doesn't. Göbekli Tepe was built before writing was invented and no one has yet claimed it was built by aliens even though it was well-planned. Apparently Aymara Indians are too dumb to stack blocks while Swiss hoteliers like von Däniken are geniuses.

The various ancient astronaut theorists (AATs) can't figure out whether the H-blocks at the site were parts of a track for launching spaceships or hinges for giant temple doors. Whatever. This material has been gone over many times, as have the Colombian gold bee and bird sculptures that they insist are actually model airplanes. These are suggested to be the crafts launched from Puma Punku. Even if they are, it still doesn't mean aliens, only that Colombians figured out how to make gliders. Not exactly rocket science.

H-Block and H-Bombs

The destruction of Puma Punku is attributed to a flood caused by a meteor strike "several thousand years ago." Since the site isn't that old, this whole segment is fruitless speculation built upon lies. The fact that bits of the building stones are mixed with the soil is taken as evidence of an "artificial blast" in the remote past or an alien nuclear war, rather than the actual cause: bits left behind from finishing the stones *in situ* and later destructive efforts at the site, human and seismic. Childress brings up his proven lies about nuclear weaponry in the *Mahabharata* to support this view. But if I understand this correctly, the AATs are saying that an explosion at Puma Punku blew the site into tiny little bits, but this same explosion spared most of the rocks there and left many of them completely untouched, including all of Tiwanaku proper right next door. Sure it did.

So, the AATs conclude that the aliens blew up Puma Punku to prevent anyone except AATs from discovering their secrets or utilizing their advanced technology, which, I guess, must not have used any metal or plastic since no advanced alien technology remains. Even abandoned sites destroyed by explosions preserve some trace of the activities of the people who lived there. If we can figure out what the people of Göbekli Tepe ate 10,000 years ago, surely there ought to be even the smallest trace of this alien technology—a dead battery, a broken chip of plastic, a lost screw—anything. But there isn't, and do you know why? It's because the aliens exist only in another dimension, the one contained entirely within AATs' imaginations.

EPISODE 7:
ALIENS AND BIGFOOT
MARCH 23, 2012

EPISODE REVIEW

Watching this, I thought: This has to be a joke, right? Like when *South Park* had *Ancient Aliens and Thanksgiving* on their "Very History Channel Thanksgiving" episode?

I guess not. "Aliens and Bigfoot" really is about the possibility that Bigfoot—and other cryptids—are extraterrestrial species that came to earth with ancient astronauts.

We start off with the supposed, and frequently debunked, evidence for the Yeti, Bigfoot, etc., including graphics apparently lifted from corporate-cousin History show *Monster Quest* and testimony from cryptozoologists. There isn't much worth discussing here since the remote possibility that large, apelike creatures exist has no bearing on the question of extraterrestrials or ancient history.

Freelance music journalist and Fortean author Nick Redfern suggests that Bigfoot is in fact a "phantom" (some kind of trans-dimensional being), and from there we hear speculation about whether Bigfoot has "ghost powers," invisibility powers, or the ability to teleport when confronted by humans and/or bullets.

David Childress, who, unbeknownst to me, wrote a book about Bigfoot, asks: "You have to wonder if Bigfoot himself isn't some kind of extraterrestrial." Remember: Childress was still insisting as late as 2011 that he was *not* an ancient astronaut theorist.

From here, the program talks about some actual history: widespread myths of "wild men" at the edge of civilization. While these are clearly stories of savage, uncivilized tribes, "ancient astronaut theorists" (AATs) say these are really encounters with Bigfoot—even though many of the wild men are traditionally described as small or misshapen. (Baby Bigfoot?)

> "There were giants in the earth in those days; and also after that, when the sons of God came in unto the daughters of men, and they bare children to them, the same became mighty men which were of old, men of renown."
>
> GENESIS 6:4

Philip Coppens then suggests that the Nephilim, the fallen angels of the Bible (Genesis 6:4) and the *Book of Enoch*, are in fact Bigfoot. The Nephilim had sex with earth women and produced "giants," but there is absolutely no connection between these giants (large-sized humans) and Bigfoot, an ape. In fact, in the King James version of Genesis 6:4, the word "giants" is a mistranslation of Nephilim, and there aren't giants at all. Even the editors seems to recognize this, jamming in a Giorgio Tsoukalos statement that has been repurposed from an earlier episode to falsely support this weird theory. In the last centuries BCE, Jewish apocalyptic tradition demonized the characters of Mesopotamian myth as monstrous Watchers (fallen angels). In the various versions of the fragmentary *Book of Giants*, both Gilgamesh and the giant he slew, Humbaba, appear as giants/Watchers. This is hardly independent confirmation of alien genetic engineering, only that the Jews set themselves apart from their neighbors by turning their neighbors' myths into Jewish demons.

We then discuss Enkidu, the wild but human companion of Gilgamesh, though the program shows an image of Humbaba, with his characteristic face made of coiled intestines, instead. Tsoukalos conflates the hairy Enkidu with the giant Humbaba (two very different figures) and claims that Enkidu was an extraterrestrial giant (he is never called a giant in the *Epic of Gilgamesh*), and Childress states that Enkidu is a "monster." Jason Martell, a web designer and self-proclaimed expert on Sumer and its "advanced technology" from "Planet X," falsely states Enkidu is the "first fashioned being by the gods"—he is not. The gods made humans much earlier, from blood and clay, as I will discuss more below. Where does he think the prostitute Enikidu sleeps with comes from? Or all the people of Uruk, the city beside his forest? Also worth noting: the *Epic of Gilgamesh* and the creation myth are not Sumerian texts, but later Assyrian and Babylonian texts that in turn drew on, combined, and embellished earlier, disconnected, and fragmentary Sumerian stories. This does not bode well for an "expert" on Sumer.

> "Create now a rival (?) to him [Gilgamesh], for the time when his heart shall be [* * *],
> Let them fight together and Uruk [shall be the spectator?]!"
> Upon hearing this Aruru created in her heart a man after the likeness of Anu.
> Aruru washed her hands, took a bit of clay, and cast it on the ground.
> Thus she created Enkidu, the hero, a lofty offspring, the possession (?) of Ninib.
> His whole body was covered with hair; he had long hair on his head like a woman;
> His flowing hair was luxuriant like that of the corn-god.
> Contrary to [?] the custom of the people and of the land, he was clothed with garments, as god Ner;
> He ate herbs with the gazelles.
> He quenched his thirst with the beasts.
> He sported about with the creatures of the water.
> EPIC OF GILGAMESH, trans. William Muss-Arnoldt (adapted)

Enkidu is quite clearly a symbolic figure meant to represent humanity in its wild state, before civilization and religion. Just as Gilgamesh is two-third god, Enkidu is his opposite and equal, two-thirds wild. We know this from the *Epic's* second tablet, excerpted in the box above at right. Enkidu only becomes fully human when a prostitute seduces him and civilizes him.

We then hear tell that Bigfoot is a devolved leftover of an alien slave-race who were of giant stature. Goliath from the Bible was probably an E.T., and apparently also the wizard Merlin. This is because they are described as large, wild men. I fail to see the connection to aliens, and worse the oldest manuscripts (the Dead Sea Scrolls) give Goliath's height as 6'7"; only later did he get exaggerated to nine feet. But the racial/ethnic/spiritual Other is always described as monstrously large. Not to be too earthy about it, but even today many white people insist on viewing African Americans, especially males, as hulking, bestial, and possessed of outsized body parts. This does not make them aliens, only the objects of racism and xenophobia.

Next up, documentary filmmaker Linda Moulton Howe and some other "investigators" talk about the astounding connection between UFO sightings and Bigfoot. Could Bigfoot ride to earth on UFOs? Well, no. The connection is simpler: UFOs and Bigfoot sightings tend to take place in the backwoods, for two reasons: 1) there are fewer people around to contradict witnesses' testimony, and 2) this is where there is a greater concentration of less educated, more credulous people.

At this point, halfway through the show, I became extremely bored. I don't believe that the aliens, who earlier in the hour had their pet Bigfeet (Bigfoots?) engaging in battles and mating with humans, now intentionally hide Bigfoot from us in vast, worldwide underground cave systems because we can't handle the truth. But ancient Israelites could?

When some cryptozoologist or another suggested that Bigfoot's "sulfur" smell is the same as Lucifer's and that Hell derives from Bigfoot's underground alien caves, I gave up. But then when Giorgio

Tsoukalos tells us that Greek mythology contains a race of "troglodytes" I nearly lost it. There are no troglodytes in Greek myth, much less troglodytes who "came down from the sky." There are only a couple of mentions of troglodytes in ancient literature, and they are from history, not myth. (Not that Tsoukalos knows the difference.) The Troglodytes are the (human) inhabitants of Troglodytis, a city, in Flavius Josephus (*Antiquities* 1.15.1) and are otherwise people who live along the Red Sea coast.

> "Now, for all these sons and grandsons, Abraham contrived to settle them in colonies; and they took possession of Troglodytis, and the country of Arabia the Happy, as far as it reaches to the Red Sea."
>
> FLAVIUS JOSEPHUS, *Antiquities* 1.15
> (trans. William Whiston)

The term originates as *trogodytes*, whose exact meaning is unknown, but probably reflected a Greek attempt to transliterate the name of a people of the Red Sea coast such as the Tuareg. This was later altered by the Greeks to troglodytes based on a folk etymology from *trogle*, or cave. Hence, cave men. The word was used in ancient times to refer to the peoples of the Red Sea. Only much later did it become a catch-all term for ugly, little cave-dwelling monsters.

But, no matter, we have Soviet chimp-human hybrids to discuss! There was a Soviet experiment to see if humans and chimps could be hybridized, and Philip Coppens doesn't seem to understand that Illya Ivanovich Ivanov's experiments failed and it isn't possible to hybridize humans and chimps through sex—thus, in the "remote past" "our ancestors" weren't making sexy monkey warriors.

Tsoukalos next claims that artistic depictions of hybrid creatures, such as animal-headed gods, are evidence of alien genetic engineering since, as is well know, human imagination was born only with Erich von Däniken in 1968. (Apparently, the aliens are all Elder Things from *At the Mountains of Madness*, releasing shoggoths on a benighted world.) He is blissfully unaware that Medusa, with her snakes, cannot be traced back to a primeval snake-headed hybrid, but is instead a complex and multivalent image, sometimes drawn after the head of Humbaba (whose face of intestines becomes the writhing snakes of the Gorgon), sometimes drawn as a dragon, and sometimes as a horse. The woman with snake hair image is very late, the result of an attempt to tone down the monstrousness of Greek monster in the Classical and Hellenistic periods.

Medusa (right) as horse-monster, early Archaic Boetian vase. (Wikimedia Commons)

Serious question for ancient astronaut theorists: *When did the aliens give us imaginations?* Since AATs claim that the "ancients" recorded alien encounters uncritically right up until 1900, as stated in Episode 1 of Season 3, "Aliens and the Old West," it must have been after that. Since Erich von Däniken claimed that he used his imagination to fancifully embellish *The Gold of the Gods* (1972), it must have been before then. Is that what Roswell was all about?

> *"In German we say a writer, if he is not writing pure science, is allowed to use some dramaturgisch Effekte—some theatrical effects. And that's what I have done."*
>
> ERICH VON DÄNIKEN, *Playboy* interview, 1974

> The Anunnaki worked the mould [for making bricks], their bricks were ...
> In the second year [the shrine was as high as] a hill, and the summit of E-Sagila reached the [celestial] Ocean.
> They made the ziggurat ......
> ENUMA ELISH 6.46-47
> (trans. E. A. Wallis Budge)

The solution for why the aliens made or brought Bigfoot can supposedly be found in "the Sumerian stories of the Anunnaki," which is ridiculous because there are *no Sumerian stories of the Anunnaki*. They are a collective of gods invoked as a group, with no mythology of their own, no epics, etc. And it is utterly false to claim that the Anunnaki made Bigfoot as a slave race because they didn't want to work, for in their only major appearance in ancient texts (the Babylonian *Enuma Elish*), the Anunnaki themselves *work* to build the city of Babylon *brick by brick,* making the mud bricks one by one with their own hands. They are not lazy plantation owners. That's just Zecharia Sitchin's false translations and fantasies repeated uncritically.

Speaking of uncritical thinkers: "Right after we shed out furs, for millennia we had to keep warm by wearing furs ... Something doesn't make sense," Tsoukalos exclaims, blissfully unaware that humans evolved in tropical sub-Saharan Africa c. 150,000 BCE, not, as the images on-screen suggest, Ice Age Europe of 10,500 BCE. Jason Martell seems to think that the "missing link" doesn't exist because aliens skipped over it in genetically manipulating us. He says that Sumerian myths say that the gods found an apelike creature and realized they could transform him into "our likeness." I don't have a clue what he's talking about. Enkidu is not genetically modified, and the Mesopotamian creation myth has men made from clay and blood, not apes. The relevant passages are at right.

For comparison, here's Berossus, the Babylonian priest, on the same:

> For, the whole universe consisting of moisture, and animals being generated therein, the deity above-mentioned took off his own head: upon which the other gods mixed the blood, as it gushed out, with the earth; and from whence were formed men. On this account it is that they are rational and partake of divine knowledge.

"I will solidify blood, I will form bone."
"I will set up man, 'Man' [shall be] his name."
"I will create the man 'Man.'"
"The service of the gods shall be established, and I will set them (i.e., the gods) free.
"I will make twofold the ways of the gods, and I will beautify [them]."
"They are [now] grouped together in one place, but they shall be partitioned in two."
Ea answered and spake a word unto him
For the consolation of the gods he repeated unto him a word of counsel [saying]:
Let one brother [god of their number] be given, let him suffer destruction that men may be fashioned.
"Let the great gods be assembled, let this [chosen] one be given in order that they (i.e., the other gods) may be established."
— ENUMA ELISH, tablet 6

Aruru washed her hands, took a bit of clay, and cast it on the ground.
Thus she created Enkidu...
— GILGAMESH, tablet 2

Yup, that sure sounds like genetically engineering humans from apes to me. It does to David Childress, anyway, who says:

> Our ancient ancestors here may well be in a sense aliens from some other solar system, perhaps the Greys. What they've done is manipulate what were already humanoids on this planet, brute humanoids.

But everyone agrees that nobody has ever found or captured a Bigfoot. This, naturally, does not mean the obvious, but rather that Bigfoot is either transdimensional or protected by aliens.

Why is Bigfoot so elusive? the program asks. That's easy: because it doesn't exist.

EPISODE 8:
THE DA VINCI CONSPIRACY
April 6, 2012

EPISODE REVIEW

As an Italian-American, I've always taken a certain amount of pride in the accomplishments of Leonardo da Vinci, so it is somewhat personally insulting to hear that one of history's greatest geniuses was nothing but a puppet of the aliens who gave him all his ideas. This is profoundly disgusting and an insult to the very idea of human imagination, made worse coming as it does almost 560 years to the day since his April 15, 1452 birth. Oh, and by the way *Ancient Aliens* title-writers, his name was Leonardo. "Da Vinci" is a descriptor, not a surname. Didn't the aliens tell you that?

To be quite honest, this episode was pretty boring for most of its run. There was a larger than usual amount of truth in this episode, relying heavily on real scholars and actual facts and insistent repetition of a few ideas time and again. There isn't much to talk about on the crazy alien front until near the very end.

We begin with a brief *précis* of Leonardo's life with a summary of his universal genius in art, sculpture, mathematics, optics, etc. that relies on actual historians and scholars, and, sadly, the almost-certainly fake Ph.D. Sean-David Morton, still described as a Ph.D. in the on-screen graphics. Then we start moving into the land of the wacky. Apparently Leonardo painted the Medusa as a clue that he was in thrall to the aliens since Medusa was an alien. Sigh.

More exciting: Leonardo used "non-lead-based paint" in one painting—which was "some type of message" according to Giorgio Tsoukalos. Seriously? This is what we have come down to? "Non-lead-based paint" is now evidence of aliens? Apparently, Tsoukalos believes that because this type of paint doesn't photograph under x-rays, Leonardo must have known this and planned for ancient astronaut theorists to fantasize about him 500 years later.

David Childress, who repeatedly has insisted he is *not* an ancient astronaut theorist mind you, then claims during the undocumented years of Leonardo's young life he was secretly being tutored by an alien-worshiping cult, or worse: "Perhaps like the biblical prophet Enoch he was even taken aboard a spaceship, and the aliens showed him earth from above and gave him a concept of the cosmos and machines and inventions..."

This is sad and disgusting. Even *Ancient Aliens* recognizes that the Renaissance was chock-a-block with geniuses and that not all of them could be extraterrestrial pupils. Afterward, Isaac Newton, Thomas Jefferson, Thomas Edison, and Albert Einstein are linked as fellow adepts whom the aliens secretly tutored to "advance" humanity "every few hundred years or so." Aliens don't, apparently, care much for people who don't speak English, or non-whites; for some reason those peoples were denied the alien genius. We get democracy, light bulbs, and relativity. All they got were big rocks and thunder myths. It doesn't seem like a fair trade, to be honest.

The ancient astronaut theorists obsess over whether mirrors can be used to reveal hidden messages in Leonardo's paintings. By mirroring his paintings and crashing the reflections together howsoever they like, the show makes pictures of Darth Vader and a Grey alien, thus "proving" Leonardo had hidden images of aliens in his work. Sadly, you can do this with any picture you like. On the next page you'll see the show's version, complete with altered eye colors followed by one I made from a completely "random" image. Recognize him? Yup, it's a young Tsoukalos. See, using *Ancient Aliens*' own methodology, you too can prove Giorgio Tsoukalos is an alien.

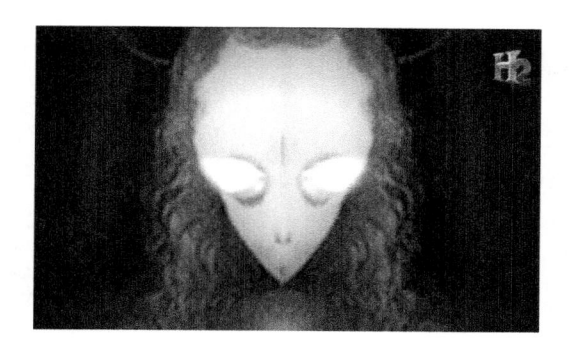

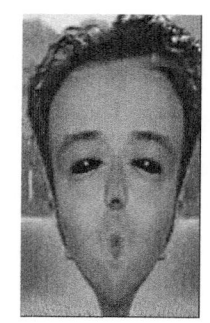

Season Four **151**

The show then wonders if Leonardo's grotesques—a well-known Renaissance genre—proves he had met real aliens because no one could possibly have made weird images without meeting aliens. (Gargoyles anyone?)

Ancient aliens, Childress said, not only helped Leonardo but also guided Columbus to the New World (Columbus had seen strange lights in the sky), thus proving again that aliens hate brown skinned people and wanted them all dead.

We then get a review of the best-of-list of UFO Renaissance artwork, primarily paintings of heavenly crowns and angelic chariots.

Aert de Gelder's *Baptism of Christ* is used as an example of a UFO in art. But a close reading shows that the "UFO" is actually a circle of light surrounding the Holy Dove, symbolizing God, and beams of light descend from this circle of light to Christ below. No UFO there— but *Ancient Aliens* doesn't play fair; they Photoshopped Gelder's work to make the circle of light appear to be a solid "spaceship" instead of the ethereal crown of light it is in the original. The original is on the facing page at left. Now compare to *Ancient Aliens*' version at right.

Oh, and this isn't a Renaissance painting. It was made in 1710.

I won't bother with any more of these paintings. Massimo Polidoro's expert debunking of this took place in 2005 and can easily be found online.

Pressing ahead, the program speculates without merit that Leonardo's inventions and unrealized plans were given to him by aliens. This is not just false but actually wrongly attributes to Leonardo the invention of automatons, something that the Byzantines had already been using in the Middle Ages on the magnificent throne of the emperors at Constantinople. Such automatons likely existed long before (Homer describes those built by Hephaestus, the blacksmith god), so in this case, Leonardo's was the culmination of a tradition, not the invention of one.

David Childress then states that "You have to wonder if Leonardo da Vinci wasn't doing this in secret because he was being encouraged by some kind of extraterrestrial masters who are somehow behind him." No, no you don't.

We finish up with the absurd claim that Leonardo was obsessed with nature because he discovered a star gate in a cave, letting him teleport to the future to steal the plans for the technologies he then pretended were his own inventions. If these ancient astronaut theorists know so much about it, how come they can't show us these star gates? Not even one?

If we take both of *Ancient Aliens'* claims at face value, that Leonardo traveled through time to the future to steal the plans for his inventions, and also that "all" our modern technology derives from Leonardo's own designs, we then end up in a time-travel paradox that would seem to imply that this knowledge appeared *ex nihilo*.

This is nothing but more of the ancient astronaut theorists' insistent claims that imagination does not exist, that creativity is a fraud, and only they—the ancient astronaut theorists—have true intellectual gifts. Everyone else got it from the aliens.

Shouldn't we check to see where these theorists are getting their ideas from?

EPISODE 9:
THE TIME TRAVELERS
April 27, 2012

EPISODE REVIEW

In this episode of *Ancient Aliens* we discuss the question everyone has been asking: are ancient aliens really "humans coming from our own future" or "time traveling extraterrestrials"? After all, these are the only two possibilities.

We begin with Einstein and relativity to give a science-ish cover to the episode by relying on actual physicists who discuss Einstein's theories and their relationship to time travel near the speed of light. Naturally, this leads directly to Hitler, just because no alien documentary is complete without Hitler. Einstein, the show claims, accidentally helped Hitler build a time machine in Poland between 1943 and 1945 by "revealing" relativity 40 years earlier. Whatever.

Conspiracy theorist Jim Marrs, author *Rise of the Fourth Reich*, has nothing very interesting to say, and Mike Bara, an alien theorist with very little connection to reality, then argues that the Nazis invented a time machine shaped like a bell and disappeared into an alternative time line. Could Bara join them? It would seem like the people who are so certain about these ideas ought to go and build one of these time machines they profess to know exactly how to make and leave this timeline in peace.

A 1965 fireball in Pennsylvania is then suggested to be a Future Space Nazi according to Marrs because the UFO sighting involved with this crash claimed the UFO (conveniently not available for inspection) was the same bell-shape as the Nazis' alleged time machine. Also shaped like bells: Bells.

But that's not all. We have more Nazis to go. Now we talk about how the Nazis went to Tibet in search of the origins of the Aryan race (detailed in the very good and serious book by Christopher

Hale called *Himmler's Crusade*) but actually discovered *time travel*. Journalist Philip Coppens talks about how the Buddhists saw time as cyclical, and David Childress (who wrote a book on time travel back in the 1990s) tells us that Buddhist stupas are the same shape as the Nazi time machine. Coincidence?! Yes. Especially since there is no Nazi time machine.

These self-satisfied theorists fail to understand that just because people *believed* that their meditations provided access to realms beyond time doesn't mean they really did. Many early faiths claimed access to realms beyond time, but this is due largely to the experience of the human mind in altered states of consciousness (feelings of timelessness), as detailed in David Lewis-Williams' *The Mind in the Cave* (2002), not to time travelers from a Nazi dimension. When meditating, on certain drugs, or otherwise in altered states, the human mind experiences self-generated stimuli that, when filtered through cultural beliefs, yield feelings of traveling to realms above or below the earth, or outside of time and space.

But now we're off to the "mysterious" ruins of Chaco Canyon in New Mexico, built between 900 and 1100 CE by the Anasazi, also called the Ancestral Pueblo. Giorgio Tsoukalos is there, dressed in a very strange combination of leather jacket and ankle-length scarf. He simply describes the ruins without anything outrageous to say. Sean-David Morton, the fake Ph.D., claims that Chaco Canyon's cities are "perfect" in shape and alignment, which they are not. Even the buildings fail to form perfect circles. Marshall Klarfeld, a follower of Zechariah Sitchin's lies, tells us that Native Americans are too stupid to build buildings, so a lost race must have built the cities instead. This is just old racist claptrap dating back to the colonial era, when the mounds of the Mississippi Valley were attributed to a lost white race. To his credit, Klarfeld doesn't say "white," but the anti-aboriginal idea is still there.

Ancient Aliens fails to understand that nearly every ancient religion, including the Anasazi, viewed creation as having multiple dimensions. Christianity has three: hell, earth, and heaven. These dimensions are related to altered states of consciousness, which at various points produce feelings of sinking below the earth or rising into the sky. This is not a literal record of traveling into the sky.

But such thoughts are beyond ancient alien theorists. Tsoukalos sees a petroglyph of a shaman holding a circle inscribed with smaller circles and declares it a map of our "spiral galaxy." It is just a series of concentric circles, probably a shield. It isn't even a spiral. Then we talk about the "ant people" of the Hopi, a mythic hybrid race, with William Henry, the investigative mythologist who invited me on his radio show and then never aired the interview. Henry believes that the secret of the universe can be found in telephone booths, which are esoteric symbols for wormholes used by Jesus to travel the universe. I am not making this up, though his major claim is about wormholes and star gates (yes, just like in the movie), not phone booths. He incorrectly claims the Sumerian Anunnaki derive from Hopi words meaning "ant (anu) friends (naki)," a derivation not supported by any modern linguist. This is more Sitchin nonsense. The word actually means "those of royal blood" and has no relationship to Hopi words from 4,000 years later. One might as well relate them to "anno" and "gnocchi," and claim they are New Year's pastas from Italy. "Anunnaki" is a conventional transliteration; the Sumerian term can also be transcribed as Anunna and Anunnaku, which are obviously different than the Hopi words.

Another Hopi mythological race, the wing makers, were said, Childress argues, to have come from 300 years in the future—which I guess would be 1400 CE, not "our present time," as Childress claims. If Childress wants us to take myths literally, we have to hold them to the 1400 date and not project random future dates just because. So, there you have it, Renaissance Europeans—Leonardo da Vinci?—traveled back in time to tell the Anasazi how to build kivas, which were "biodomes or biospheres made of nuts and bolts," as Tsoukalos said. The reason that the kivas of Chaco Canyon are *not* biodomes is simple: there is no glass or plastic found at the site. Where did the domes go? The kivas were actually covered with regular old roofs, and they were far too small to support an entire ecosystem, not being airtight or having any way of pumping water or air even if they were.

Next up: the *Mahabharata* from India, where the show claims "King Revati" or "Raivata" (both are used) visited Brahma and returned to find that while visiting the god hundreds of years had passed on earth. Revati is not the king's name, however. It is the name of his *daughter*. The king's name was Kakudmi, for all of you keeping score at home, though he is sometimes called Raivata, son of Revata. I am not an expert in Indian epics, but I understand that

An alien biodome, minus the dome, the "bio," and any way of using it as such. Actually, it's a Chaco Canyon kiva. (Library of Congress)

Kakudmi is only briefly mentioned in the *Mahabharata* and the story of his voyage to Brahma is actually told fully in the *Bhagavata Purana* and other later epics. Some modern commentators believed the legend emerged to account for an anachronism in the myth where an earlier and later figure had been brought together.

The show says Jeremiah in the Bible tells a similar story, but my next essay will explore in detail how this is a lie. This Rip van Winkle theme is well known in folklore (there are many other variants, including the stories of the Briton King Herla, the Irish bard Oisin, and the Japanese Urashima Taro), but ancient astronaut theorists think that this represents time travel due to special relativity. This theory was first proposed by Japanese sci-fi author Aritsune Toyoda. Instead, such myths talk about the timelessness of the gods, and how for them a thousand years are like a day. This isn't time travel but a recognition that the immortals are exempt from the normal flow of time. This is a logical outgrowth of the development of gods who are immortal and in the cosmic level above earth; it is not a literal representation of time travel or Einstein's special relativity. The idea derives, probably, from the recognition that when we sleep time moves differently in dreams; months or minutes might pass in our minds while eight hours march forward in reality. Once again ancient astronaut theorists believe ancient people are too stupid to have created their own ideas; all it takes is imagination, not alien science.

Besides, the *Bhagavata Purana* tells us that when Kakudmi returned to earth, he found that the people had shriveled and become stupid. Since there is no evidence of a race of genius giants, there is no reason to take the rest of the story as fact either.

William Henry restates Robert Temple's long-debunked and completely false *Sirius Mystery*, seconded by Philip Coppens, claiming that aliens from Sirius came to earth and gave us our civilization, including anomalous knowledge of the Sirius system. It's been more than twenty years since anthropologist Walter van Beek proved that the supposedly alien-derived knowledge of Sirius recorded in Temple's book was a fraud, and yet ancient astronaut theorists continue to repeat these claims as though they were true.

We then move on to discussions of modern physics and what it can tell us about time travel, which might be interested in another context but is mostly just filler here. Supposedly we will have a working time machine in ten years, according to a physicist whose name I didn't catch, but sadly this time machine will work only on a single neutron at a time. Henry returns to talk about wormholes, but he knows not whereof he speaks, claiming falsely that the Dendera temple of Hathor depicts time travel portals because ancient Egyptian boats are shaped like wormholes. Obviously a boat must be a wormhole and not, as it appears to be, a boat to ferry the gods across the sky. This is wrong for many reasons, not least of which is the fact that our depiction of wormholes as essentially U-shaped is purely a conventional shape to represent an idea—in reality, if such things exist, they would take any number of shapes, assuming that it is possible at all to depict in a two-dimensional shape a space existing in two realms across four (or more) dimensions.

I admit that at this point we are getting into cosmological discussions beyond my understanding of physics, and clearly beyond the show's understanding, too. Giorgio Tsoukalos sums up just how little he knows about physics, ancient history, and, well, everything:

If you place a picture side by side of the Hadron Collider and the Aztec calendar, there is an eerie similarity between the two. The Aztec calendar was known to be a gateway to the universe, and the Hadron Collider is similar to that because we are trying to unlock the secrets of the universe with this machine. And I find it fascinating that we have a carving from a long time ago and when compared with the modern day Hadron Collider there *is* an eerie similarity. Is it coincidence? I think not.

They are similar only in that they are both concentric circles. You know what else has concentric circles? The ripples made by a rock falling into a pond. Captain America's shield. The Hopi petroglyph Tsoukalos identified as "our spiral galaxy" in the last episode. The program then combines images of the Hadron Collider and the Aztec calendar (right) and makes the calendar rotate as though to reinforce the idea that it depicts the Hadron Collider. Of course the collider is *not* a flat circle. That is one image taken from one angle. The actual collider exists in three dimensions.

Aztec calendar. (Library of Congress)

We finish up with UFOs and alien abductions, with the well-worn trope that the Grey aliens (earlier discussed as aliens in a previous episode) are in fact *future humans*! The coincidence of humanoid shape has nothing to do with travelers from the future and everything to do with the fact that humans are inventing human-like creatures.

Childress claims the Roswell incident happened near the birthday of the goddess Isis, so therefore the aliens are really "some kind of time traveling extraterrestrials." No, I do not understand the connection either, except that the narrator tells us that the aliens probably came from Sirius via teleportation (in the words of Edgar Mitchell, the ex-astronaut). So, they are smart enough to come from another star system by advanced super-technology on a specific day relative to the apparent position of that star in the sky relative to the earth and then dumb enough to crash their ship into the desert near Roswell.

Philip Coppens disagrees and states that the Greys are actually future humans who lost the ability to procreate and have returned back in time to have sex with us. This is mostly just a rehash of the material from the earlier "Greys" episode of *Ancient Aliens* (see p. 81). Apparently time travel didn't have enough material to fill out the hour, so a bit of repetition was needed.

The program closes with a false dichotomy, asking if ancient gods were future human time travelers or extraterrestrial beings and if we can ever know for sure.

Remember, those are your only choices.

COMMENTARY
INVESTIGATING BIBLICAL TIME TRAVEL

IN INITIALLY REVIEWING "The Time Travelers," I let pass a brief discussion of time travel in the Hebrew Bible because (a) I wasn't familiar with the story and (b) assumed that the producers of the show would have done the minimal amount of research to quote the Bible correctly. The story concerned the prophet Jeremiah and what was essentially an early version of the Rip van Winkle story. I didn't think this was really worth commenting on, but after discussing it with Biblical scholar Mike Heiser on Twitter, I learned from Heiser that the story isn't in the Bible at all. Naturally, I decided I had to investigate yet another case of *Ancient Aliens* fraud.

Here is the case of biblical time travel as given in "The Time Travelers":

> *Narrator:* And in the Hebrew Bible descriptions of the prophet Jeremiah in Jerusalem are eerily similar to both of these [Japanese and Indian] accounts of time travel.
>
> *Erich von Däniken:* Even in the Bible the prophet Jeremiah was sitting together with a few of his friends, and there was a young boy. His name was Abimelech. And Jeremiah said to Abimelech, 'Go out of Jerusalem. There is a hill, and collect some figs for us. The boy went out and collected the fresh figs. All of sudden Abimelech hears some noise and wind in the airs [sic] and he became unconscious—he had a blackout. After a time, he wakes up again, and he saw it was nearly the evening. So, he runs back to the society, and the city was full of strange soldiers. And he said, 'What's going on here? What happened to Jeremiah and all the others?' And an old man said, 'That was 62 years ago.' It's a time travel story written in the Bible.

Pretty much nothing in this statement is true. It also wasn't true when von Däniken first made the claim in 1977's *According to the Evidence: My Proof of Man's Extraterrestrial Origins*, though back then he apparently knew more about the story than he does now. Let's begin at the beginning.

First, this story is not found in the Bible, Hebrew or otherwise. The story is contained in 4 Baruch, also known as *Paraleipomena Jeremiou* ("Things Left out of the Book of Jeremiah"), a pseudoepigraphal work—meaning it was not written by the person named as the author. It was written probably in the second century CE, and the story contained in it is not found in other pseudoepigraphal texts of Baruch (such as 2 Baruch, on which it is dependent), indicating this story was created at a very late date. Let me stress: *this book is not part of the Bible*. The story is meant as a fantasy, allowing the author to fill in the back story of what transpired during the period in which Abimelech is gone, and it continues on to describe how the figs were brought to Babylon and used to end the Babylonian captivity. The entirety of the text is designed to console the Romanized Jews about the loss of the Temple and to prophesy its swift reconstruction following Hadrian's expulsion of the Jews in 132 CE.

N.B. Today von Däniken claims that source is the Bible, but in 1977 he claimed the source was "*The Remains of the Words of Baruch,* or as it is also called the *Addendum to the Prophet Jeremiah*," which he called "ancient Jewish scriptures." This appears to be a variant translation (probably on the part of the English translator of von Däniken's German text) for an alternate title of 4 Baruch, *The Rest of the Words of Baruch*, the title used by J. Rendell Harris in editing the text in 1889 but not otherwise common. Von Däniken's description would be accurate if the text were (a) Jewish (it's a Jewish-Christian hybrid), (b) scripture (it's not canon), or (c) ancient (it's nowhere near as old as, say, Genesis).

The story is also told in a different but related apocryphal text, the Coptic *Jeremiah Apocryphon* (possibly third or fourth century CE), in which Abimelech sleeps for seventy years beneath a mountain (!) and picks both grapes and figs. This, therefore, was not von Däniken's source as these details do not appear in his description.

Second, there is no wind or noise. Abimelech states clearly that he fell asleep in hot weather and then woke up. The text states clearly that he was "preserved" by the spell of an angel, just like King Arthur, Odin, and Cronus in a widespread European myth of the sleeping king. (There were other sleeping hero myths in the Near East as well.) Perhaps significantly, Abimelech's name means (in one translation) "my father is king" and was the title of Philistine princes.

Third, there were no soldiers; and fourth, it was not 62 years but 66.

Reading the full text of 4 Baruch (available freely online in modern translations) shows that it is little more than a Rip van Winkle fairy tale pressed into the service of Jewish politics circa the second century CE. If you don't believe this book is a fantasy, perhaps the rest of the story left out by von Däniken can make the case: A magic eagle takes the figs to Babylon, where they have gained the supernatural power to raise the dead. Later, Jeremiah dies and is resurrected. During his "death" he becomes convinced of the truth of "messiah Jesus, the light of all the ages" and delivers a prophecy of the coming of Christianity. Then the Jews stone him to death.

So, unless we are prepared to believe in magic eagles and death-defying figs (a spaceship delivering alien technology, I suppose), I don't see any reason to reinterpret Abimelech's sleep as Einsteinian time dilation. If we do that, then why not Sleeping Beauty or Snow White? Snow White was even in a glass coffin, which is *clearly* a cryogenic chamber. *Did the medieval European peasantry have cryogenic chambers? Folklore says* YES!

So why do ancient astronaut theorists ignore fairy tales but embrace pseudo-historical fables?

And, more importantly, why does it take this much research to explain just one thirty-second-long lie on *Ancient Aliens*?

EPISODE 10:
ALIENS AND DINOSAURS
MAY 4, 2012

EPISODE REVIEW

I HAVE NO IDEA how to review this. There. I said it. This is so stupid that I am at a complete and total loss to make coherent sense out of the stupidity in this episode, not the least of which is the simultaneous claims that dinosaurs were killed off by aliens 65 million years ago but were also alive to walk with humans at some unspecified more recent date. This is the episode that told us that the aliens negotiated with fish, and it is the episode relying for evidence on at least three long-debunked claims as though they were real.

We begin with the discovery of dinosaur fossils in the early nineteenth century and a brief review of what dinosaurs are and how they lived from real scientists. This is filler. Then Philip Coppens tells us how dinosaurs are "to some extent supernatural creatures," and David Childress tells us that "everything was gigantic" in the past—which is not true. Many things were giant, yes, but mammals, for one thing, were very small.

Almost a quarter of the way in, we finally get to the aliens. Jason Martell says we don't know where dinosaurs came from—implying outer space. Apparently evolution escapes him. Giorgio Tsoukalos, who sometime before this episode began promoting himself online as the "author" of a PowerPoint presentation, says that because the age of dinosaurs is a thousand times longer than that of humans "dinosaurs are by far the dominant species in the history of this earth," which is false on two counts: first, dinosaurs are not a species but many species, not all of which lived simultaneously; second, they didn't "rule" the earth in a literal sense. If being the paramount predator for a long period makes a species dominant, then the first single-celled amoeba-like predators that happily ate other cells for the first billion years of life must be the most successfully dominant "species" using Tsoukalos' wildly inaccurate definition.

Tsoukalos then suggests that prior to the early nineteenth century, no one would have believed giant creatures roamed the earth, implying that we are in a similar position today in denying the existence of aliens. This is again false. Prior to the nineteenth century, people believed in all manner of gigantic, imaginary beasts, not least of which were the biblical Leviathan and Behemoth, which creationists often wrongly call dinosaurs. Other monsters include dragons, themselves sometimes thought to possibly derive from early sightings of dinosaur bones.

So, were dinosaurs an "early experiment" by the aliens, as Tsoukalos claims? It would mean the aliens spent 150 million years working on it. That takes commitment. But even if they weren't genetically engineered, ancient astronaut theorists are fairly certain that aliens killed off the dinosaurs, possibly by sending the asteroid that caused the Cretaceous-Tertiary (K-T) boundary event. Oddly enough, *Ancient Aliens* makes no mention of the surviving dinosaurs—birds—at this point because this does not fit into their imaginary story of vengeful aliens wiping clean the earth like God and Enlil in the Flood myth. The birds will come much later when viewers are presumed to have forgotten the completely contradictory material from this segment.

David Childress, noting that the K-T asteroid struck in the Yucutan, then asks:

> You have to wonder if it's not some sort of strange coincidence that the same spot, the Yucatan, which experienced this devastating asteroid

strike which caused extinction of the dinosaurs is also the main habitation area of the ancient Maya.

No, you don't. No matter where an asteroid hit on the land surface of the earth, an ancient people would be living near it. There were people almost everywhere on earth, just as there are today. Try to find a spot in the habitable area of the earth that did not have someone living on or near it sometime between 100,000 BCE and 1500 CE. Having people living 65 million years later on a buried asteroid crater is hardly news. People were living atop Herculaneum in Italy for centuries without realizing there was a buried Roman city under their feet—and that was hardly a 65 million year gap.

So we move on to Chichen Itza, a post-Classic Maya site (meaning it is very late—1000 CE or later), and here Philip Coppens claims that the Maya built there to remember the asteroid, which is impossible. Why would the Maya wait until after their civilization collapsed to build, with the help of the Toltec, supposedly the most important site in their cosmology?

The screen then shows a Maya mural painting that includes the head of a "dinosaur" that Childress says defies explanation. It's clearly a lizard or a snake, depicted in the same style as other examples of Maya snakes and lizards. Apparently "ancient astronaut theorists" don't know that earth still has some of those around. The lizard in the picture doesn't have feathers, so the show waits to tell us dinosaurs had feathers until after we've forgotten the art.

Similarly, sculptures of serpents are also just that: exaggerated snakes. I will grant, however, that the carving on Angkor Wat's Ta Prohm temple looks like a stegosaurus at first glance. This would be the first interesting thing they've shown, had the Smithsonian not debunked this in 2009. Like many other medallions on the temple, this one shows an animal against a backdrop of stylized leaves—not bony plates on the spine. It's a rhinoceros walking through the jungle. The key is more "bony plates" that are surrounding the medallion as a whole—clearly meant to depict jungle leaves. Naturally Giorgio Tsoukalos claims this is evidence that the artist drew the stegosaurus from alien descriptions.

David Icke—he who believes Queen Elizabeth and George H. W. Bush are lizard people—shows up to suggest that serpent worship reflects reptilian aliens, backed up by Michael Bara. The ancient astronaut theorists, so quick to say that any smudge that looks like a saucer is a UFO, tells us that we have to "interpret" images that are clearly snakes to turn them into dinosaurs.

Then we go on to Glen Rose, Texas and the long-debunked claim that human footprints alongside those of dinosaurs. Michael Cremo and William E. Dye—both creationists, Hindu and Christian respectively—can tell us these are real, but that still doesn't make this decades-old hoax true. Especially clever is the way the show avoids using the more familiar name for the tracks, the Paluxy footprints, to keep viewers from being able to look them up and see how fake they are.

Philip Coppens then tells us again that some dinosaurs must have survived the K-T boundary event. Yes, they did. They are called *birds*. The show will discuss these later, after squeezing all the potential out of the "mystery" they are self-creating. Instead, we get from Coppens a rant about carbon dating, which is completely irrelevant, as even the show recognizes briefly before immediately forgetting again. Carbon dating can only be used for objects up to about 60,000 years old. This is a far cry from the 65 *million* years of the youngest dinosaur fossils. Fossils, as we know, are not *organic* objects. Fossil bones have become stones. This doesn't stop Philip Coppens from complaining that carbon dating of dinosaur bones doesn't appear in peer-reviewed journals (well, duh...) and therefore science is engaged in a conspiracy to suppress the truth about dinosaur survival into historical times. Even if dinosaurs survived "thousands or even millions" of years after the K-T boundary event, this changes history exactly how? They would still all be dead 60-63 million years before humans.

Next: The Ica Stones! These are so fake I won't bother to even review them. Just read the *Skeptic's Dictionary* entry on them. Note particularly that the "dinosaurs" depicted on these modern forgeries show only dinosaur species known in the 1960s, as they were depicted in that era, without feathers. Creationist William E. Dye confuses "Ica" and "Inca" and claims the Inca rode dinosaurs to work on the basis of the stones.

But apparently we can't fill out an hour with just dinosaurs, so we instead go on to sci-fi speculation about what would happen if asteroids hit the earth today, followed by a rather dull discussion of the asteroid that hit at the K-T boundary event. This becomes enlivened when the narrator suggests aliens used nuclear weapons around the world to destroy the dinosaurs. The evidence is that dinosaur bones are radioactive, which Michael Bara says is due to alien nuclear bombs. It is in truth due to the fact that the bones fossilized in sediments rich with carnotite—a uranium-bearing ore, meaning that the bones soaked up uranium and turned into uranium-rich stone. This is not a mystery or a conspiracy and is well-documented in the scientific literature.

Jason Martell tells us that the *Mahabharata* describes the mass extermination of giant lizards, and the on-screen images show asteroids pummeling diplodocuses. However, in the actual ancient text, this is not at all what happens. In one passage, Arjuna battles a giant crocodile—which is clearly stated to live in the water, not on land. The crocodile then turns into a beautiful woman. Additionally, the giant lizards, where they appear, occur with "countless beasts of gigantic size, and stags, and monkeys, and lions, and buffaloes, and aquatic animals" (Vana Parva 145). This does not sound at all like dinosaurs when placed in context—just the usual exaggeration of heroic deeds common in myth.

Michael Cremo lies about "advanced technology such as spacecraft" in the Indian texts, something predicated on how seriously one takes claims of flying chariots; and Tsoukalos lies about "weapons of mass destruction" in the *Mahabharata*. He is paraphrasing the completely fake quotations I exposed a long time ago as utterly and completely false. (The modern myth, discussed on my website,[7] derives from the purposeful conflation of separate passages of the ancient text and the falsification of their translation.) Repetition does not suddenly make them true.

Finally: Birds! Nice of the show to acknowledge well-established science as it grinds toward its conclusion; however, they are wrong that Archaeopteryx is the "only" dinosaur that could fly. There are many birdlike dinosaurs known. Seriously, does anyone bother to do even cursory research? It was in *National Geographic*, for crying out loud. But, apparently, it is not enough to say that humans were

---

[7] See "The Case of the False Quotations" at JasonColavito.com/the-case-of-the-false-quotes.html

genetically engineered by aliens. Apparently they also genetically engineered birds, too, "as many ancient astronaut theorists believe."

"According to evolution, all dinosaurs are died out about sixty millions of years," Erich von Däniken states ungrammatically. "So the question is why only the dinosaurs died?" Evolution is not a book; it is a theory, and it makes no such claim. He is also wrong that "only" dinosaurs died out in the K-T extinction. Many species of plants and invertebrates also became extinct. It is the largest animals—the non-avian dinosaurs—that suffered the greatest losses because they were, well, biggest and ran out of food fastest when the plants died.

Much hay is made of the fact that the coelacanth, a large fish, survived from prehistoric times even though humans thought it had gone extinct millions of years ago. (It had a good hiding place—the bottom of the ocean.) Tsoukalos states that "I think it is possible that the coelacanth survived due to a direct guarantee by extraterrestrials." They make treaties with fish?! WTF?! Is this some weird thing like when *Star Trek IV* had aliens communicating with humpback whales? Seriously, though, to whom does he imagine the aliens were making this guarantee? Tsoukalos thinks the aliens—and I can't possibly make this up—preserved the DNA of coelacanths, turtles, crocodiles, and sundry other animals, cloned them following the mass extinction 65 million years ago, and then reintroduced them when it was time to make themselves some human slaves.

And with that freakish image of ancient aliens negotiating the future of the earth with coelacanths, this episode and Season Four wheeze to an inglorious conclusion.

APPENDIX
RÉSUMÉS OF THE GODS

I'M THE LAST PERSON to argue that one needs a Ph.D. to be able to write intelligently about ancient history. I certainly don't have one, and I like to think that my work is worth reading. But a passing familiarity with the methodology of archaeology and historiography would certainly seem an important prerequisite for claiming startling new interpretations of prehistory that would overturn centuries of carefully scholarly work.

So, I took a look at the talking heads on *Ancient Aliens* to see how their background prepared them to critically evaluate the past two centuries' worth of archaeological research, including changing theoretical frameworks and methodology.

Does it surprise anyone that not a single ancient astronaut theorist appearing on the program has specialized training in archaeology, anthropology, or history, or even an undergraduate degree in these areas? (Exception: alternative historian Graham Hancock has a degree in a somewhat related field.) Here's what I've learned about some of the talking heads who appeared in the third and fourth seasons of *Ancient Aliens*.

(Note: *Ancient Aliens* also mixes in professional archaeologists and historians, but these individuals do not endorse the ancient astronaut theory and are not discussed here.)

Giorgio Tsoukalos
- Former bodybuilding promoter
- Bachelor's degree in sports information communication
- Demands a "positive light" clause in interview contracts

David (Hatcher) Childress

- One year of college education
- Falsely claimed to be an archaeologist in *Extraterrestrial Archaeology* web video
- Was sued for copyright violations and settled out of court

Erich von Däniken

- Former Swiss hotelier
- No known educational background in history, archaeology, etc.
- Convicted of fraud, sued for plagiarism, diagnosed as "compulsive liar"

Philip Coppens

- Journalist, almost exclusively writing on alternative and conspiracy theories
- No known educational background in history, archaeology, etc.

George Noory

- Radio talk show host, *Coast to Coast A.M.*
- Bachelor's degree in Communications
- Former law enforcement training video manufacturer

Sean-David Morton

- Self-described psychic medium
- Charged with fraud for allegedly swindling clients out of $6 million
- Claims doctorates in theology and psychology that cannot be verified

Graham Hancock
- Alternative historian rather than ancient astronaut theorist (but: see his *Mars Mystery*)
- Bachelor's degree in sociology
- Journalist and international correspondent for many major newspapers

Brien Foerster
- Former marine biologist
- Professional sculptor and outrigger canoe salesman
- No known educational background in history, archaeology, etc.

Chris Dunn
- Craftsman and machinist
- Human Resources Manager, Danville Metal Stamping
- No known educational background in history, archaeology, etc.

Michael Bara
- Aerospace engineer
- Conspiracy theorist
- No known educational background in history, archaeology, etc.

The question is: Why are no professional historians and archaeologists ancient astronaut theorists? If Carl Sagan could flirt with the idea, it can't be that it's *prima facie* stupid. The answer must be that *there is no evidence for it and anyone with actual training in history or archaeology recognizes this fact*.

I'll reiterate that one does not need a degree to say something worthwhile about a subject. Barbara Tuchman was a journalist and wrote one of the most famous histories of the run-up to World War I, *The Guns of August*. David J. Skal is recognized as a cultural historian of horror despite having no Ph.D., and S. T. Joshi is the foremost scholar of Lovecraft, but again without a Ph.D. But all of these scholars knew what they were talking about, understood the fundamentals of their field, and drew on the best of academic work to craft their own.

Ancient astronaut theorists have no such respect for archaeology or history as disciplines, only as means to an end: proving a preconceived notion.

INDEX

AAS-RA. *See* Ancient Alien Society
Abimelech, 165, 166, 167, 168
Akhenaton, 63
Aldrin, Buzz, 119, 120
Al-Maqrizi, 28
Ancient Alien Society, x, 6
Ancient Aliens, 4, 1, ix, xiv, xv, 5, 6, 7, 9, 11, 12, 21-28 *passim*, 33, 35, 36, 41, 43, 47, 48, 51, 54, 57, 59, 60, 63, 64, 67, 73, 81, 86, 88, 91, 93, 94, 97, 101, 106, 114-116, 119, 120, 124, 127, 129, 137, 149-153 *passim*, 157, 159, 164, 165, 168, 172, 179
ancient astronaut theorists, xv, 6, 8, 9, 21, 24-28 *passim*, 33, 35, 41, 42, 47, 48, 51, 57, 58, 60, 64, 67, 70, 76, 81, 82, 84, 85, 88, 94, 95, 97, 111, 112, 115, 116, 133, 134, 137, 143, 150, 153, 161, 162, 168, 172, 173, 174, 177, 181 (See also under individual theorists.)
ancient texts, 22, 24, 28, 36, 68, 73, 75, 86, 96, 143
Anunnaki, 24, 25, 26, 27, 28, 103, 105, 132, 143, 159
Apollo missions, 15, 87, 119, 120, 122
Archaeology, Aeronautics, and SETI Research Association. *See* Ancient Alien Society
Assyrians, 25, 75, 139
At the Mountains of Madness, 122, 142
Atlantis, 123, 131
Aztecs, 105, 130, 163

Babylon, 25-28 *passim*, 105, 143, 166, 167
Babylonians, 17, 18, 25, 51, 67, 75, 94, 103, 105, 113, 139, 143, 144, 166
Bara, Michael, 120, 122, 124, 157, 174, 175, 181
Bauval, Robert, 121
Berossus, 144
Bigfoot, 137, 138, 140, 143, 145
Blavatsky, Helena, 52, 106, 107
Bolon Yokte, 96
Book of Enoch, 138
Brad Meltzer's Decoded, 47
Bramley, William, 51-54 *passim*
Brotherhood of the Snake, 51-54
Burke, Edmund, 43
Chaco Canyon, 158, 160
"Charioteer of the Gods," xiii, xv
Chariots of the Gods?, 23, 25
Charlemagne, 59, 82, 88
Charroux, Robert, ix
Chicago Reader, xiv
Chilam Balam, Books of, 96
Childress, David (Hatcher), ix, xiv, xv, 21, 22, 33, 36, 37, 57, 64, 74, 83-85, 88, 97, 101, 103, 104, 111, 112, 114, 119, 121, 124, 129, 130-133, 137, 138, 145, 150-152, 158, 160, 164, 171-173, 180
China, 21, 111
Christianity, 85, 159, 167
Coast to Coast AM, 6, 21, 74
coelacanths, 177
Contagion, 5

Coppens, Philip, 82, 87, 105, 113, 130, 138, 141, 158, 162, 164, 171, 173-175, 180
Cowboys & Aliens, 5, 6, 9, 11, 47
Cremo, Michael, 112, 174, 176
Crowley, Aleister, 122
crowns, 15, 18, 151
Cult of Alien Gods, 1, ix, xiii, xiv, 114
Däniken, Erich von, ix, xiii, 23, 24, 28, 83, 84, 87, 105, 116, 121, 130, 132, 133, 142, 143, 165-167, 177, 180
Dead Sea Scrolls, 140
dinosaurs, 106, 111, 171-177
DNA, 104, 105, 108, 177
Dogon, 114
dragons, 86, 87, 107, 142
Dunn, Chris, 130, 181
Dye, William E., 174, 175
Easter Island, xv, 21
Eden, 23, 24, 51, 53, 107
Egyptians, ix, xv, 16, 25, 27, 53, 63, 120, 122-124, 162
Einstein, Albert, 150, 157, 161
El Castillo, 95
elongated skulls, 101, 104
energy grid, 57
Enkidu, 138, 139, 144
Enoch, 150
Enuma Elish, 25, 58, 75, 143-144
Epic of Gilgamesh, 138-139, 144
extraterrestrials, xiv, 5, 6, 15, 22, 34, 35, 36, 37, 41, 42, 51, 52, 57, 60, 63, 76, 85, 88, 111, 113, 114, 122, 127, 132, 137, 157, 164, 177
Foerster, Brien, 130, 181
Founding Fathers, 47

Freemasonry, 122
Freemasons, 47
Fuente Magna Bowl, 131
Gelder, Aert de, 151, 152
Genesis, 58, 74, 86, 138, 167
Gilgamesh, 87, 113, 138, 139
Golden Dawn, 122
Great Pyramid, 57
Greeks, xi, 15, 35, 52, 59, 67, 68, 69, 70, 85, 87, 104, 112, 120, 132, 141, 142
Grey Alien-Coelacanth Peace Treaty, 177
Greys, 44, 63, 101, 102, 106-108, 145, 163, 164
H2, ix, xiv, 81, 91, 93, 101, 130
Hammurabi, 17
Hancock, Graham, 113, 121, 179, 181
Heaven's Gate, 51
Heiser, Mike, 165
Helios, 15-17
Henry, William, 159, 162
Hephaestus, 34, 152
hieroglyphs, 85
Hill, Betty and Barney, 101
History Channel, ix, xiv, 5, 6, 9, 10, 47, 101, 129, 137
Hitler, Adolf, 157
Hittites, 67
Hopi, 94, 103, 159, 163
Howe, Linda Moulton, 140
Ica Stones, 175
Icke, David, 54, 106, 124, 174
Jeremiah (prophet), 161, 165, 166, 167
King Arthur, 34, 167

Index 185

kivas, 160
Klarfeld, Marshall, 158, 159
Köfels Impact Event, 94
K-T Boundary Event, 172, 174, 175
Kukulkan, 86, 94
Landsburg, Alan, 81, 88
Legendary Times, 24
Lemuria, xiv
Leonardo da Vinci, 149, 150-153, 160
Lewis-Williams, David, 69, 158
Lovecraft, H. P., 1, 122, 182
Machu Picchu, 57
Mahabharata, 33, 35, 133, 160, 176
Marduk, 25, 26, 75, 103
Marrs, Jim, 157
Mars, 105, 119-121, 123, 124, 181
Martell, Jason, 103, 139, 144, 171, 176
Maya, xv, 21, 52, 59, 64, 81-88, 91, 93-97, 115, 173
Medusa, 142, 149
Mesopotamia, 24, 27, 53, 75, 105, 113
Milky Way, 91
Minoans, 67
Mitchell, Edgar, 119, 164
Morton, Sean-David, 91-94, 115, 149, 158, 180
mummies, 63
Musgrave, Story, 119
Mycenaeans, 67, 69, 132
NASA, 6, 117, 119-124
National Academy of Sciences, 7
Native Americans, 131, 158
Nazca, 23
Nazis, 123, 157, 158
NBC, xi
NBCUniversal, 6
Neanderthals, 63
Nebuchadnezzar, 74, 75
Nephilim, 138
Noory, George, 6, 21, 74, 106, 180
Oannes, 94
Old West, The, 5, 6, 9, 12, 143
Olmec, 84
Osiris, 120, 122
Pacal, 82, 83, 84
Paluxy Footprints, 174
Planet X, 139
Playboy, 84
Popol Vuh, 86
Poseidon, 69, 112
Posnansky, Arthur, 127-129
Prometheus Entertainment, xv, 6, 9, 10, 41
Puma Punku, 88, 127, 129-134
Quetzalcoatl, 94, 106
Ra, 16
Rainbow Serpent, 43, 87
Romans, 15, 16, 59, 82, 86, 105, 120, 123, 130, 173
Satan, 74, 106
Scientology, 74, 113
Secret Doctrine, 52
Sirius Mystery, 114, 162
Sitchin, Zecharia, ix, 24, 28, 51, 64, 75, 103, 132, 143, 158, 159
Sol Invictus, 16
Star of Bethlehem, 48
Stonehenge, 132
Sumerians, 24, 25, 51, 52, 74, 75, 85, 103, 113, 131, 132, 139, 143, 144, 159

SyFy, xi
Temple, Robert, 94, 114, 162
Teotihuacan, 57, 105
Theosophy, 106, 107
Thor, 34
time travel, 103, 108, 157, 158, 161, 162, 164, 165
time travelers, 108, 158, 164
Tiwanaku, 88, 127-130, 133
Tower of Babel, 28
troglodytes, 141
Tsoukalos, Giorgio A., ix-xv, 6, 11, 12, 15, 21, 22, 24, 27, 28, 33, 34, 37, 41, 48, 68, 73, 74, 83-87, 95-97, 101, 102, 105, 113-115, 127, 130, 132, 138, 141, 144, 149, 150, 158-160, 162, 163, 171, 172, 174, 176, 177, 179
Twelfth Planet, 28
Twitter, 73, 165
UFO, 23, 57, 58, 101, 103, 114, 120, 121, 124, 140, 151, 157, 174
UFOs, 57, 103, 111-113 *passim*, 119, 121, 140, 163
vampires, 51, 60, 63, 74, 85
volcanoes, 113, 114
Washington, George, 47
Zeus, 34, 67, 87, 120, 123
ziggurat, 25, 26, 28, 57

ABOUT THE AUTHOR

Jason Colavito is an author and editor based in Albany, NY. His books include *The Cult of Alien Gods: H. P. Lovecraft and Extraterrestrial Pop Culture* (Prometheus, 2005), *Cthulhu in World Mythology* (Atomic Overmind, 2012), and more. His research has been featured on the History Channel, and he has consulted on and provided research assistance for programs on the National Geographic Channel (US and UK), the History Channel, and more. Colavito is internationally recognized by scholars, literary theorists, and scientists for his pioneering work exploring the connections between science, pseudoscience, and speculative fiction. His investigations examine the way human beings create and employ the supernatural to alter and understand our reality and our world.

Visit his website at http://www.JasonColavito.com and follow him on Twitter @JasonColavito.

Printed in Great Britain
by Amazon